On Angels' Wings

My Life as a Healer

On Angels' Wings

My Life as a Healer

Pamela Russell

&

Barry Russell

AYNI BOOKS

Winchester, UK
Washington, USA

First published by Ayni Books, 2013
Ayni Books is an imprint of John Hunt Publishing Ltd., Laurel House, Station Approach,
Alresford, Hants, SO24 9JH, UK
office1@jhpbooks.net
www.johnhuntpublishing.com
www.ayni-books.com

For distributor details and how to order please visit the 'Ordering' section on our website.

Text copyright: Pamela Russell & Barry Russell 2012

ISBN: 978 1 78099 679 0

Design: Stuart Davies

Printed and bound by CPI Group (UK) Ltd, Croydon, CR0 4YY

We operate a distinctive and ethical publishing philosophy in all
areas of our business, from our global network of authors to
production and worldwide distribution.

CONTENTS

"This book is dedicated in loving memory
of my husband David Russell,
who always encouraged me in healing and writing."
Pamela Russell

Wings of an Angel

Angels descend in a rainbow of colours
As travellers gaze from one to another
Angel wings giving warmth and love
Beings of light giving guidance from above
White feathers falling at your feet
Showing you the way
Each and every day
Living life to the full
Being strong, walking tall
Hear the sound, hear the call
Guided gently by the wings of an angel

A whisper in the air
A fragrance, a touch
A breeze through your hair
As the wings of an angel
Caress you
Inspire you
Encourage you
Knowing you are never alone
An aura of gold a shimmering tone

Pulsating white lights like a shooting star
Rainbow of colours from afar
Just as the day is dawning
A glimpse of the future
A gentle warning
Soaring up into the sky
On the wings of an angel you can fly

I was awoken by a shrill cry, not knowing if it was myself or my mother who had screamed. I had fallen asleep by the open fireplace and my arm had dropped in to the burning embers of the fire. My mother raced to my side and began desperately pulling the red hot cinders from my arm with her fingers without thought for her own safety. While this was happening I remember my older brother Ronnie returning home from the store proudly holding his brand new toy. Even with all the commotion I remember feeling sorry for him as my mother made him give me the toy to calm me down and distract me from what was happening. In shock and pain I was rushed to the hospital. The next thing that I remember was being treated by the doctor and my arm had been bandaged and put in a sling. Despite the seriousness of my injury everyone was amazed to find that the burns had left no marks or scarring on my arm. It was as if it had never happened at all. I think even from a young age someone was watching over me and protecting me from harm. It was not until later in life that I understood the significance that this guidance would have on my life.

On the 26th of July 1946, my mother gave birth to me in our

home, a small council house on Pear Tree Gardens in Dagenham, Essex. Back in the forties childbirth was a very different experience for expectant mothers and home births without any form of pain medication were not unusual. Rather than go to the hospital, a Midwife came to our house to deliver me. I was christened Pamela Elizabeth Doreen Dabbs. The third of four children, sister to Ronnie, Ricky and Roy. My mother was born in Newcastle in 1914, one of eight children. By the age of eighteen, the scarcity of work led to her leaving the area in search of new opportunities. Fiercely independent, she travelled to London alone and found employment as a house maid in Dagenham, working for a family called the Faimens. It was during this time that she met my father, the local postman. They would routinely meet as she collected the morning mail from him, which led to friendship, courting and eventually marriage. My father continued to work for the post office for forty years, initially as a postman before eventually working his way up to become the treasurer of one of the country's largest post offices. He was always very well respected within the local community and became a point of call for anyone in the area in need of help with any kind of paper work. He also developed a reputation for his mental arithmetic skills. He always believed that he could total up numbers much quicker in his head than using a calculator. Family, friends and colleagues often enjoyed firing random series of numbers at him to try and catch him out but to no avail, he would always arrive at the correct answer before anyone had finished inputting the numbers on the calculator. My father's mathematical prowess was all the more impressive as he had suffered from rheumatic fever as a child and missed a great deal of schooling. His joints were so badly affected he could barely move his fingers and would practice 'walking' them up the walls to exercise them. Despite being too ill to attend school he continued his education by arranging to have books brought to him by the local library. He taught himself maths independently and I'm sure his life would have been extremely different if he had not taken this upon himself. I strongly believe that with positive thinking and willpower there is nothing as individuals that we cannot overcome and nothing that can stand in the way of someone determined to fulfil their life's purpose and dreams.

Newcastle remained an important part of my early life and we would always visit the family on my mother's side every year. Even at my tender age I knew this was an entirely different way of life to what I was used to. My four uncles were all miners working down the pit, which provided jobs for most of the local men living in that area. My Grandmother's house had a large stove in the front room and yet the home was kept spotlessly clean. Despite not having much she was very house proud and made sure everything gleamed and sparkled. She also handmade a great deal of the clothes and outdoor coats that the family wore. It was a very different time back then and I always remember that none of the front doors along the street were ever locked. If you wanted to visit someone you would just open the door and walk in and yet there was always a feeling of being safe there. I cannot imagine a community operating in such a way in this day and age. What I loved the most about visiting our family was an overwhelming feeling of how peaceful and quiet life was there and waking every morning to the sound of birds singing. These are things that I still value in my life to this day.

Time upon Tyne

The air was filled with thick black smoke
As miners in the coal dust choke
Their backs near breaking, their aches and pains
Slag heaps looking like large black stains
Through cobbled streets where no one could hide
 The washing stretched from side to side
The pit wheel turning around and around
As glowing lamps reflect across the ground
Not a key was turned, not a door to lock
Just the still and the quiet of a ticking clock

From the age of four I began taking ballet lessons and appeared in several ballet shows over the following years. There were several examinations for me to pass as part of my continued development and training. I remember one time scoring 99% from the examiner in an important end of year exam. My teacher congratulated me and said that I must have practiced very hard in order to achieve this, although I knew full well that this was not the case. Rather than physically practicing the routine, I would lay in bed just before going to sleep and go through the whole piece in my mind. Visualising myself performing every single aspect of the dance flawlessly. I later found out that the 1% that I lost from my score was because I had forgotten to smile, something I had not considered during my visualisations. I strongly believe that the process of visualising yourself accomplishing your goals is an integral part of achieving success and every bit as important as practicing. I believe this to be true of all aspects of life not just in terms of memorising a routine. If there is something you wish to achieve in your life it is extremely beneficial to imagine yourself having already attained your final objective.

At the age of eleven my teacher had taken me as far as she could and I was offered the opportunity to continue my ballet studies at the famous Sadler's Wells Royal Ballet School. The school has a strong international reputation receiving applications from all over the world. However as it was a residential boarding school this would have required me to leave home and live at the onsite accommodation. At this young age I was very shy and I did not want to leave my family and live with strangers. I never regretted turning down the fantastic opportunity that I had been offered however I did later regret not sticking with ballet beyond this point. My current teacher had offered to train me as a teacher myself, but as an eleven year old girl I just wanted a normal life. I had been focusing on ballet for 7 years already and decided that I wanted a break from it all and be able to have fun with my friends without the pressure of continual study.

When Karma Calls

Let the love from your heart flow
Let the joy from your soul glow
Like a light spreading across the ground
As your heart sings its sweet sound
As Karma calls knocking on the door
As you pick yourself up off the floor

A sparkling drop of rain
To wash away the pain
Upon the earth, show no fear
Give your love, not a tear
Spirit of the earth is free and wild
Laughing loudly like a child
So be positive, be bold
It's what you give unto the world
That returns to you ten fold
A beacon of light, an aura of gold

The world is yours for the making
The world is yours for the taking
Giving you love or drama
Creating peace or Karma

Let the love from your heart flow
Let the joy from your soul glow
Like a light spreading across the ground
As your heart sings its sweet sound

When I was fourteen years old I had the first, of what would turn out to be many, very strange experiences. I was walking to the local shops, which required me to cross a small street and then a very busy major road. I approached the small street and then all of a sudden I found myself on the opposite side of the busy road with no knowledge of how I had got there. I felt absolutely stunned and embarrassed as I looked around for some kind of explanation. How could I have possibly crossed these busy roads without any knowledge of it happening. This was the first time that I had been exposed to something so unusual and I decided to keep it to myself, fearing people might not believe me. It was not until much later that I began to make sense of this incident, and realise that I was not the only person to have experienced these circumstances. This is what I refer to as a Time Warp. Although often discussed in science fiction, a Time Warp is based on real world science and refers to Einstein's theory that time and space form a continuum that warps or bends relative to gravity. This can result in lost time or more specifically being able to travel to a destination faster than would be physically possible. There have been numerous cases of people who have experienced time warps in times of need when they are running late and have called upon Archangel Metatron to aid them. Archangel Metatron, often referred to as the angel of thought, has great insight in to the flexibility of the universe and the nature and manipulation of time and space.

At the age of eighteen, after experiencing terrible pain and discomfort in my back and sides and feeling very weak and fatigued, I went to visit the local doctor, who in turn sent me to the hospital. After being seen by a doctor I learned that the source of my malaise was a kidney infection. I was given some medication and sent home with an instruction to rest. One night shortly after this, as I lay in bed, I felt as if I had suddenly become paralysed. I couldn't move a muscle and began to panic, I didn't understand what was happening to me or if this would be permanent. I then experienced a sensation of floating up out of my body towards the ceiling. From my new vantage point I was able to look down at my own body still lying lifeless in the bed. Now terrified of what was happening, I desperately tried to get back to my body. I tried to pull myself closer by grabbing at the bed covers, but then realised that I could not touch or move them. As I struggled to think what to do next I heard a voice proclaiming to be my Aunty Jean. I answered that I didn't have an Aunty Jean and I just wanted to get back to my body. I then felt a sharp jolt and the next thing that I knew I was back in my bed, now able to move freely. Like my earlier unusual experiences I decided to keep this information to myself out of embarrassment and fear that people would think I was making these things up. Not long after this I had another similar experience. Whilst lying in bed I once again felt myself rising up out of my body, although this time I felt less panicked. Without any control of where I was heading, I floated from my bedroom all the way down the stairs and back up again to my body still lying on the bed. It felt more relaxing and almost dreamlike this time, as though I was looking at the world through a window as if not really there.

Many years later I was looking through very old family photos that I had never seen before with my mother. As she showed me the photos, she explained to me who all the old family members in the pictures were. One photo featured a middle aged woman in a clean white apron and a slim, pretty young girl in a black dress with a white frilled collar. The older woman was my Great Grandmother. My mother told me what a lovely woman she was and when she visited her as a child her Grandmother would wash my mother's waist long hair and then sit her on the back of a lamb to let her hair dry in the wind as the lamb raced around the garden. I do not know much about the young woman next to her in the photograph other than her name. I was shocked when my mother told me that that she was my Great Auntie Jean. It was then that I realised who had called out to me that night several years before, and yet still I said nothing about our encounter to anyone. It was much later in life that I heard of 'out of body experiences' and realised that this had in fact happened to other people as well. The term 'out of body experience' was actually used to distance researchers from the issue of the human soul, something notoriously difficult for scientists to explain, and be able to discuss the experience in more scientific terms. However, these experiences can also be referred to as Astral Projections, which stems from the philosophical works of Plato. This suggests that in addition to our physical body we have an astral body which is capable of travelling separately in the astral plane. The astral plane has been described as "The point where Heaven and Earth meet" as discussed in Camille Flammarion's L'atmosphère: météorologie populaire (Paris, 1888).

More and more strange things seemed to be occurring in my life at this point, seemingly without explanation. One night while trying to get to sleep I felt my bed suddenly start to shake violently as if at the epicentre of a earthquake. My bedside lamp and other objects in my bedroom were also shaking wildly. I could not explain the cause of this and worried that perhaps it was a ghost, like a scene out of a horror movie. Too frightened to leave the room I hid under my bed covers until it was over and remained there until morning. None of my family felt or heard anything unusual in the night and once again I believed that I couldn't tell anyone about the weird and frightening things that were happening to me, as I felt sure they would not understand and they might judge me harshly. It was not until much later that I discovered that rather than a ghost, it was my own energy that caused this event to happen. I was using my own subconscious mind to make things move and shake within my room. Without realising it I had been releasing a very powerful energy. Unknowingly there had been a strong build up of energy inside me that had no release or direction and as a result manifested itself in this form. I now know that this phenomenon was in fact telekinesis. Later in life I learned how to focus this energy in a more positive way but at the time I had no idea what was wrong with me for so many crazy things to be happening in my life.

At the end of 1968, at the age of twenty two, my best friend Barbara and I were invited to her brother's New Year's Eve party. Once at the party I met a friend of her brother's and we got on very well. Some people called him Dave, and others called him David. I asked him which he preferred and he just smiled at me and said that he didn't mind. So from that moment on he became my Dave. We became good friends and started dating. As our relationship progressed and developed I was introduced to his family: his father Alec, mother Marjorie and his brother Peter. They were all very nice and made me feel very welcome in their home. Just over a year after meeting, on the seventh of February 1970, Dave and I were married at St. Mary's church in Dagenham. I remember walking out of the house in my wedding dress to the hired wedding car and looking up to see Dave in his car drive past me on his way to the church. Some people think it is bad luck for the groom and the bride to see each other on the morning before the wedding, but that is not something that I have ever believed in. I just marvelled at the coincidence that his car happened to be driving past our house just at the moment I had left the house. I could just as easily have left the house one minute earlier or one minute later and not seen him travel past, but we happened to be in the same place at the same moment which I took to be a good sign. I do not believe that coincidences are merely chance encounters but are in fact destiny. Everything in life is meant to happen and happens for a reason. As our driver parked the car at the church I was helped out of the back seat and gazed at the church realising just how large it really was. It was a very windy winter's day and my head dress blew right off my head and flew away. My father had to run right down the street to catch up with it so I could reattach it. As I entered the church I was overwhelmed by how packed with people it was including lots of our neighbours, friends and family, including all my relations from the north, who completely filled all the pews. I walked down the aisle to where Dave was standing waiting for me and our life together as man and wife began.

Our first home together was in a house in Gidea Park that was split into two separate upstairs flats with the landlord occupying the downstairs area. The flat consisted of a lounge, a small bedroom, a kitchen/diner and shared a bathroom with the couple in the other flat. In the bathroom, the toilet was positioned in the centre of the room and you had to climb up three steps to get to it. As a result I jokingly referred to it as 'The Throne Room', which always made people laugh, especially once they had seen it. On our very first day in the flat we managed to lock ourselves out of the kitchen. Rather unusually it locked as you shut the door, and unfortunately we had left the keys in the kitchen and had no means to get in. Dave decided to climb out of the hallway window and walk along the top of the house and then get back in through the open kitchen window. I desperately didn't want him to do this as it had been snowing and couldn't bear the thought of him slipping from the roof. As he climbed up, I just stood and prayed that he wouldn't fall and hurt himself, or worse. My thoughts were interrupted by an ear splitting scream. My heart racing and fearing the worst, I approached the window. But before I could get there a terrified cat dived through the window giving me the shock of my life. Dave had clearly disturbed the cat as he made his way to the roof and it had been the cat that had made the screaming noise I had heard. By the time I had caught my breath, the kitchen door opened behind me revealing Dave, to my great relief. In hindsight I'm sure it would have been easier if we had just asked the landlord if he had a spare key.

During our time at Gidea Park, Dave worked as an assistant foreman on a building site and I worked for a window company with my mother on the opposite side of the street from him, so Dave and I could travel the long journey to work together. Dave needed to be at work much earlier than I did so I would eat some breakfast and have some coffee in the work kitchen before I was due to start work. The people were all really kind and friendly and it was a very nice place to work. Although, one day I was called to my boss's office to be informed that another staff member had made a complaint about me coming in early and 'making myself at home'. I explained to my boss that Dave started work earlier than me and this way we could travel to work together. My boss didn't actually mind at all and told me not to pay any attention to the person making the complaint. It still annoyed me that someone had made a complaint though. Sometimes people can get angry about the stupidest things and it made me realise the impact that just one person's negativity can have on you if you allow it. Although it also taught me the importance of rising above people who are just looking to cause problems for you and how this will nullify their impact on your life. There will always be people trying to project their anger or negativity on to you in life, but it's important to remember that these people are not as important to you as the people that care about you, and therefore their behaviour does not deserve your attention.

Dave and I very much wanted to leave our small flat and find ourselves a nice house to live in, but there was no way that we could afford to do this. Dave decided that one way we could achieve this was for him to apply for a job as an off-licence manager, at a shop that had an adjoined house. That way we would have both a new home and Dave would have a good job as well. Luckily Dave was successful in his application and he was offered the role of off-licence manager in Freezywater in Enfield. I was sad to say goodbye to the lovely friends I had made at work but it was time for me to move on to something new. The off-licence was situated at the front of a very old house which would become our new home. I had to get a new job as Dave was not earning enough money to keep us both. Every day I worked from seven o'clock in the morning until one in the afternoon at a factory that made tennis rackets. After this I would go home to do all the housework and cook the dinner before joining Dave in the shop from six in the evening until ten at night. Although the four hours in the shop every evening did not really feel much like work because we enjoyed each other's company so much and we liked chatting with the customers.

Nothing unusual had happened to me for some time now and I had put the previous events out of my mind altogether, instead choosing to focus on my new life with Dave in Enfield. Things continued this way for a while until one night when I woke up in the early hours of the morning while it was still dark and I decided to get up to use the bathroom. I sleepily stumbled to the hallway towards the bathroom when all of a sudden I snapped in to full alertness. I stood motionless in the hallway staring ahead in disbelief. The bathroom doorway was completely filled with what I can only describe as a large circle of bright shining colours slowly spiralling around. The beautiful mixture of colours was almost like looking at reflections through refracted glass or crystals when the light hits them in a certain way, only this was more tangible and solid looking. It was like looking through a doorway leading to another world. I was gripped by fear and had no idea what it could be. I presumed it was some kind of portal. I didn't know what would happen if I got too close to it. Could I walk through it and just disappear? For all I knew at the time I was seeing something from outer space. I quickly decided that I did not need to use the bathroom that badly after all and went straight back to bed and endured another sleepless night hiding under the covers. I was very nervous of using the bathroom in that house for some time afterwards especially if I had to get up in the night. I now felt comfortable being able to share my strange experiences, but only with Dave. It was a relief to be able to share these things with him without feeling as if I were going to be judged or thought of as crazy. Dave always accepted everything that I told him as the truth and never once questioned or doubted me.

Several years later I attended 'An Evening with Diana Cooper' in Devon. Diana Cooper is a well known healer and has written many books on the subject, as well as books on angels, spirit guides and many other aspects of spiritual life. She really is a remarkable lady and her books have been a huge inspiration to me on my own path to spiritual enlightenment. After the event I had the opportunity to speak with Diana and I described the circle of colours to her and asked her if she had any idea what it was that I had seen. She told me that what I had seen was in fact a collection of many angels. She was also kind enough to sign one of her books with a personal message for me "To Pam, Archangel Metatron is with you". If I had known what the circle of colours was at the time I'm sure that I would not have been frightened. Looking back, I wish I had stayed by the lights for longer and spent more time looking at it. I also would have asked my spirit guides what I was seeing and why it was happening to me and nobody else. Although I had no idea about angels or spirit guides at this stage of my life. In hindsight I believe that this was a group of angels who were trying to make a connection with me. Although I do not think at the time I was ready to hear their message and didn't know how to listen to them.

Another night I had been lying in bed sleeping when I was woken up by a tapping on my leg. I looked over at Dave to see what he wanted but he was fast asleep. I reasoned he must have bumped against me during his sleep, and I laid back down and shut my eyes. A minute later the tapping started again. I sat up and to my amazement I saw a very slim lady in a long grey dress walking right past the end of my bed and then disappeared through the wardrobe. She moved so smoothly it was as if she was gliding. I don't think she even noticed that I was watching her. I felt as though someone else had been tapping me in order to get my attention so that I would see her, although I did not know why. I knew I had just seen a spirit, I do not like the term ghost. I believe that when we die and move on to our next life we all become spirits, and just like people, some are good and some are bad. Despite these extraordinary occurrences happening more and more frequently I was still shaken up by them and would once again retreat beneath my bed covers and wait for the morning.

Dave and I always enjoyed a good rapport with the customers in our off-licence and it proved to be a good way to meet people and make friends in the area. One day Dave was chatting with a man who worked at a dog rescue centre and was told of a one year old black Labrador puppy called Sheba who had been brought in to them. Sheba had been treated badly by previous owners before the people at the dog rescue centre had stepped in to find her a new home somewhere safe. Later on Dave told me all about Sheba and we both felt that we could offer her a better life with us and we made arrangements to bring her in to our family. When Sheba came to live with us we decided that she could sleep in the kitchen at night, but she ended up barking the whole night through. The following night we let her sleep in the lounge, thinking she might be more comfortable there, but she barked all night again. We also tried letting her sleep at the bottom of the stairs the night after that but once again she wouldn't settle down and spent the whole night barking. On the fourth night we took her upstairs with us and let her sleep outside our bedroom door and that is where she slept every night from then on without making a sound. I think all she wanted was to be close to us.

After approximately five years of living at Freezywater, Dave was rewarded for all his hard work at the off-licence with the opportunity to manage one of the largest off-licences the company had. This meant that we would be moving to Basildon, Essex and have a lovely two floor apartment which was much larger and nicer than where we had been living before. The apartment was situated above the off-licence, and had two bedrooms which was important as I was now six months pregnant with my first child. The windows in the new flat were very large and our curtains weren't big enough, so while the removal men brought the furniture up I sat in the corner sewing our curtains together so that they would fit. Money seemed harder to come by in those days and it was important to make the best of what you had, rather than just replacing old for new.

On the 23rd of March 1976, at thirty years of age, I gave birth to my first son, Taro John Russell. After a full day of labour pains I eventually had to be induced and in the end forceps were attached to Taro's head so that he could be pulled out. Despite a difficult birth he was born healthy and he had the most beautiful blue eyes, which everyone seemed to comment on. Taro was always a very kind and thoughtful little boy. I remember being with him at a mother and baby class when he was just two years old and after seeing a little girl fall over, Taro walked over to her and helped her up and asked if she was alright. All the other mother's were watching and couldn't believe how caring he was. Taro went on to become a very independent person who would always prefer to teach himself to do things, even as a young child he taught himself to ride a bike. He always tried to be the best at whatever he did whether it was skateboarding, canoeing or playing American football. He also joined the cubs and collected every single available badge before moving on to join the scouts, which proved to be a great inspiration to me later in life when I began writing children's stories. One of the main characters in my published collection of children's stories "Tell Me a Story" was a little bear called Jolly Jingles who prided himself on being 'real life' bear cub scout.

We always enjoyed taking holidays together as a family, whether we were travelling up to Newcastle to spend time with our relatives or going on holiday with my parents. Sheba was now an important part of our family and would travel with us everywhere we went. Sheba loved to be with us and was so careful and loving around Taro. She used to let him sit on her back and ride her around the front room as a young child. When Taro learnt to walk we never had to fear if he started to wander away from us as Sheba would go after him and gently shepherd him back in our direction. The four of us went to stay in a caravan at a holiday park in Wales, with my mum and dad and my brother Ronnie. Taro was now three years old and I was six months pregnant with my second child. One night in the caravan something disturbed me from my sleep. I looked over to Dave but he was still asleep. I sat up in bed to see a man wearing a long white robe standing in the doorway. His arms were outstretched in front of him with the palms of his hands facing upwards. Immediately I knew it was another spirit that I was seeing, rather than someone breaking in, although I can't really explain why. This time, however, I did not feel scared by what I was seeing. Perhaps I was getting more accustomed to seeing such unusual things or on some level I knew that this spirit was nothing to be frightened of. I wondered why it was that this spirit had come to me. What possible reason was there for me to see this. I also felt a little frustrated, as at six months pregnant I really did not need all these strange visions coming to me. The following morning I asked Dave if he had seen or heard anything during the night but I already knew what the answer would be. I was used to being the only one to see things like this and I think Dave was getting used to unusual things happening to me. In spite of this we had a really good holiday and it was lovely to spend time with my mum and dad. My mum and dad both really loved Taro and they would babysit him every weekend. I always remember my Dad getting down on his hands and knees and crawling around on the floor with Taro riding on his back, which Taro absolutely loved. The first week we were back at home we bought a new sofa and arm chairs for the front room. I phoned my dad to tell him about it and we ended up talking for ages. It was lovely, but unusual as we never really chatted on the phone. Exactly two weeks after seeing the visitor in the long white robe, my dad died unexpectedly from a heart attack. It was all very sudden as he had not previously been ill. It was a terribly sad time for all of us and we were deeply shocked. I hadn't initially understood the connection between the man in the long white robe and my father passing away. It could so easily have been an unrelated coincidence, at least that was what I thought at the time.

The due date for my second child came and went, and I was becoming increasingly anxious as the days went by. I was now ten days past my due date and I was worried that I might have to go to the hospital and be induced as was the case with Taro. After a difficult first birth and having lost my father only three months before I was desperate to have this birth naturally and for everything to go smoothly without any complications. I had heard that walking helped the baby along, so Dave and I would walk around the car park just outside our apartment, but to no avail. I would talk to my unborn child and say "Come on. It's time now for you to see the world." I was now working my way through the old wives tales of what might naturally induce labour. I had a hot bath followed by a spicy curry at 10pm at night and fortunately that seemed to do the trick, as I started to have contractions just two hours later. We had everything prepared in advance but the one thing we hadn't counted on was our car not starting, so we had to phone for an ambulance and just three hours later my second son was born. I had originally intended to call him Ty, but after the recent death of my father I thought it would be nice to let my mother choose his name. So at 3:00am on the 4th of January 1980, Barry Richard Russell was finally brought into the world, taking my father's name as his middle name. I was taken to a hospital ward with the other new mums, but there appeared to be a lot of commotion within the ward. I was told that there was a contagious virus on the floor above so naturally I did not want me and my new baby to stay at the hospital and potentially get an infection. Shortly afterwards the doctor gave me a check up and told me that I could go home, so a paramedic drove me back home in an ambulance. I don't think anybody realised that I had just given birth a few hours earlier but I didn't say anything as I thought they might not let me go home if they knew. I made my way up the two flights of stairs with Barry in my arms and knocked on the front door of my apartment. Everyone was shocked to see me arrive home so soon, but very pleased to see me and Barry.

Barry was a very good baby. I think I had learned a lot through having Taro and I was much more prepared this time around, so things didn't seem quite so overwhelming. When I brought Taro home from the hospital I would pick him up every time he cried and cuddle him. In time he soon learned that all he had to do was cry and I would come running to comfort him. With Barry I was advised not to pick him up every time he cried if I knew he was clean and had been fed and that soon enough he would settle down on his own. I hated to hear him cry and not be with him. It went against all my mothering instincts. For the first week I would just sit on the stairs and cry when he cried. I would check in on him to make sure he was alright but not pick him up. After keeping this up for one difficult and heart wrenching week Barry would sleep right through the night without crying from then onwards. Having said that Barry was always a very mischievous little boy, but in a good way. One day when Barry was still a very young baby I went to his bedroom to get him out of his cot after being left to sleep, only to find that he was not where I left him. I looked around the room and saw him sat on top of a wardrobe playing with some soft toys that I kept on there. He had managed to pile all of his soft toys together in his cot and used it as a ladder to climb up and out of the cot and somehow made his way up to the top of the wardrobe. He became quite the escape artist and we found it very difficult to find a cot or a play pen that he couldn't climb out of. If you turned your back for a moment he was out and trying to climb the stairs. Another time I had left him strapped into a high chair for a moment with a boiled egg in front of him. When I returned I saw that he had finished but I couldn't find the egg shell anywhere, I looked all over the floor to see what he had done with it and then he said "can I have another one please mum. I like the crunchy bits best". I wrote about this and several other of his antics in "Tell Me a Story".

Some time after my father had died, I was in the kitchen making cakes as a surprise for the children. I used to bake cakes all the time back when the boys were young. I was making some butterfly cakes and thinking about how much the children were going to enjoy them. Suddenly I felt the urge to turn and look towards the doorway. Standing there in front of me, as clear as day, was my father with Taro on his shoulders. I only saw him for a few seconds and then he disappeared. I strongly believe that when someone close to you dies they come back to let you know that they are alright. Also they will often appear to you with something or someone familiar to put you at ease. This was the case with my father and seeing Taro on his shoulders. I knew right away that Taro was not actually there but it was a familiar image to me as my father always loved to play with Taro. It saddens me that he never got the chance to meet Barry as I'm sure he would have loved him just as much. I wasn't frightened by this appearance. How could I possibly be frightened of someone that I loved? I knew that he had come to see how I was, which was very comforting. I smiled and went back to my cooking, happy in the knowledge that wherever my father was, he was alright.

A Life Between Worlds

A golden trail of Angel lights
Sparkling through velvet night
Looking through thin veils
Stepping into the balance of time
Into the future, into the past
A life of actors, A life of mime
Each playing out a role
A symbol of the soul

Stepping into portals
Of mist and swirling colours
Adventures of mere mortals
Each sister and each brother

Energies flowing through time and space
Filling every cell, without a trace
Enriching each and every being
Without us even seeing

Quietening our every pace
Knowing life is not a race
The magical mind of sleep
The positive mind won't weep

Insights into our journey of life
Each hurdle without strife
Transcending into a life of dreams
Rainbows of colours, like golden beams
Angel lights like a shooting star
Comforting us from afar
A life Between Worlds

Dave now had four staff members to help him run the off-licence so I was able to spend my time in the flat with the boys. This was the first time that I didn't see much of Dave, as he was always working long hours. One day while Dave was in the shop, I was in the kitchen stirring something in the pan when suddenly, seemingly for no reason at all, flames burst up in to the air engulfing both sides of the cooker. I screamed out in shock "Oh God!". As soon as I had spoken the flames went out immediately, leaving nothing but thick black smoke marks all around the cooker. Remarkably, on closer inspection nothing in the kitchen had burned. I was left stunned, not entirely sure how to take in what had just happened. It had started and ended in such a flash I barely had a chance to catch my breath but somehow I was safe and completely unharmed. Two weeks after this happened I was cooking some chips in the frying pan, when the doorbell rang. It was my mother at the door and I was so pleased to see her that while we were talking I forgot all about the chips cooking in the pan, which unbeknownst to me had caught fire. Luckily Dave was in the flat at the time and he rushed us and the kids out of the flat and then put out the fire himself. The kitchen was badly damaged but thankfully we were all unhurt. I believe that the near miss two weeks prior was actually a sign, warning me about what was going to happen, which unfortunately I did not realise at the time. I just felt grateful that my family was safe.

Thanks to Dave's hard work, the off-licence in Basildon had now become the company's flagship store. We actually won many competitions from the company for selling the most promotional products out of all the UK based shops, which resulted in us receiving lots of prizes. We won several holidays including trips to Dublin, Copenhagen, and Paris, often staying in luxurious hotels that we otherwise could never afford. We also received prizes such as expensive crystal glasses and decanters. I remember talking to our area manager Mr. Jones who was telling me about how a couple, who were running another one of the company's off-licences a few streets away, who were so unhappy and were always complaining about their customers. I replied that we had been very lucky in that the customers in every shop we had worked in were always really nice and friendly. Mr. Jones said to me that it had nothing to do with luck and it wouldn't matter what shop or area that the other couple worked in, they would still not be happy. Whereas me and Dave were content wherever we went. He explained that it was not the shop or the area but the person in it. I feel that sometimes people wonder why bad luck seems to be following them around, but if they are a negative person then they will carry that negativity with them wherever they go. But if you can be a positive person you can, in turn, carry that with you everywhere and people will respond to that positivity.

It was a happy time in our lives but sadly nothing lasts forever. Once the road that the off-licence was situated on was closed off we realised that we wouldn't get so much passing traffic and the shop would no longer get as many customers and therefore would not get as much trade. Rather than wait to see how badly the sales were affected and fearing that this could signal the beginning of the end for the store, we decided it was time to move on. We found another off-licence with the company that Dave could manage in Rainham, Essex. The company had originally planned to have Dave take over one of the largest London shops but we were determined that we wanted to be in Rainham and eventually the company yielded and gave us what we had asked for. At the same time that we were moving, my mother and my brother Ronnie were also moving in to a flat in Rainham. Having family nearby was a major factor in choosing the shop that we did. Before they moved we went over to see them while they were packing. It was a very strange experience as it was our family home and I had lived there for the first twenty three years of my life and it would be sad to leave it behind for good. As I walked in to the lounge it felt different although I couldn't put my finger on what it was that had changed. I ran my hand across the wall for where the fitted cupboard was but it wasn't there. I felt all around the wall looking for where the cupboard should be but the area was completely smooth and the wallpaper in that area looked new. I knew for certain that the room had not been redecorated and the cupboard blocked in and yet I could not see it. I looked all around the room trying to make sense of why the cupboard was no longer there. We didn't stay much longer and I decided not to mention it to anyone, after all I knew the cupboard must still be there but for some reason I just couldn't see it. When we arrived home I decided that for my own piece of mind I would call my mother and ask her about it. She laughed and said to me "of course the cupboard is still there. I certainly don't have time to redecorate, I'm too busy packing". I pretended that I had only been joking and didn't mention the room as I had seen it, as I didn't want her to worry about me. Afterwards I felt even more confused than before. A fortnight after they had moved in to their new flat I received a call from my mother telling me that they had forgotten to unpack the cupboard in the lounge leaving behind many treasured possessions and all my ballet certificates. She couldn't understand how she had managed to forget to unpack it. I believe that two weeks prior I had in fact seen the room as it was now that the new family had moved in, with the cupboard sealed up and wallpapered over. It's such a shame that I didn't realise that I was being sent a warning to make sure we unpacked it. Sadly it was too late to do anything about it now. It was now becoming clear to me that for some time I was being sent messages and warnings and that I would have to pay more attention to what I was being told.

We had all settled in to our new home very well and Sheba enjoyed playing with the children, although she would run away and hide when they tried to ride on her back. I think she was perhaps getting too old for that now. In the new home she had made the spot outside our bedroom door her own just as she did in the previous house. One night I woke up and felt very thirsty and had to carefully step over her as I made my way downstairs to get a glass of water. When I reached the bottom stair I looked up towards the kitchen and standing in the doorway was the man in the long white robe, once again with his arms outstretched in front of him and the palms of his hands facing upwards. I wish I could say that this time I felt brave enough to approach him and ask him questions, however, I just turned around and went straight back to bed, deciding that I could go without the water after all. I described what had happened to Dave the following morning, but neither of us understood the significance of seeing the visitor. Tragically two weeks after seeing the man in the white robes my brother Ronnie died as a result of a fire. It was a terrible shock for the whole family. I had now seen the man in the white robes twice and two weeks after-wards on both occasions a loved one had unexpectedly passed away. It was now that I understood that the man I had seen was sent as a warning to prepare me for what was coming. In my mind, I asked not to see this man ever again as the warnings would be too distressful for me and thankfully that was the last time I saw him. Although not the last time that I received warnings of significant events to come.

One morning, as I had just woken up, I was sitting on the edge of the bed when I noticed everything around me becoming misty as if I had just walked in to a dense fog. In front of my eyes events played out before me as if I was watching a movie, except with no sound. I saw a tunnel that went through a mountain and lots of men were working on it wearing hard hats. It was as if my eyes were the movie's camera and I looked over the edge of the mountain and saw astoundingly beautiful scenery. Land, grass and trees as far as I could see in several different colours and hues. I turned back towards the tunnel and went inside. I saw some kind of a lever being pulled and then the tunnel began to collapse around me and filled with smoke. I rapidly backed out of the tunnel as the whole thing collapsed and then all I could see was the smoke, which gradually faded and once again I was sat in my bedroom. It was frustrating to see this but not to know where this place was or if there was a reason for me seeing this. I had no idea whether or not this was some kind of a warning but with the limited information I had at my disposal there was no way of knowing.

One afternoon I saw Sheba lying in the stock room which was just behind the shop. I knew something was very wrong with her. She hadn't touched her dinner so I mashed up some of her food in to my hand and she gently licked it. We decided to see how she was as the day went on and then take her to the vets if she still seemed ill. While she wasn't well we spent a lot of time stroking her and giving her lots of attention. My uncle Ken, who was visiting from Newcastle, went with Dave to take Sheba to the vet a little bit later. Sadly that was the last time that I ever saw Sheba. It was terribly sad for us as Sheba had always meant so much more to us than just being a pet. She was an important part of our family and one of a kind. She was greatly missed by us all.

An Eagle's Eye

Flying free across the sea
An eagle glides on a breeze
Spreading knowledge, wisdom and love
To the earth looking down from above
A frozen world stood alone
Looking like a lifeless stone
An inkblot or a blackened stain
The planet began rotating again
A shuddering and splintering of ice
Like the spinning throw of a dice
As the ice began to melt
A new meaning to life was dealt
Moving into universal orbit
A glowing candle was lit
Bringing a warmth back to life
For every man and his wife

Signs of change
Times to rearrange
A new beginning to an end
Of harmony and love to send
Echoing across the lands
Illuminating golden sands
As the earth trembled and quivered
Breaking ice shimmered and slivered
The eagle soared up through the sky
On the crest of a wave he could fly
The sky stretching into infinity
Wings flapping with a look of serenity
Fire, water, earth and air
Flying high without a care
Seeing a vision across a crystal maze

An eagle's eye a defiant gaze
A jewel flickering in a flame
An eagle eye too wild to tame

One day in the off-licence a local couple came in and Dave and I got talking to them and we found out that they had a young boy with muscular dystrophy. He was in a wheel chair but what he really needed was an electric wheel chair. They told us how impossible the situation was because the cost of the electric chair that their son needed was much more than they could afford. Afterwards Dave said to me that he wanted to lose some weight as he had recently become overweight which wasn't good for his diabetes, so he suggested that we combine the two things. He decided to try and raise money for the young boy's electric wheel chair by getting sponsored to lose weight and we would ask each customer who came in to the shop if they would sponsor him. The customers thought it was a great idea and it proved to be a great success even getting reported by the local newspaper. It was hard work but in the end Dave received enough sponsorship money to buy the little boy his electric wheelchair and lost all of the weight that he needed to in the process.

I would always take my son Barry to playschool in the mornings and one day I noticed how badly they needed new tables and chairs for the children. I spoke to Dave about this and he decided that we should do something about it to help out. Dave formed a group of likeminded people and we called ourselves 'The Rainham Fundraisers'. We knew that there was a local fun run taking place soon so we decided to wear fancy dress outfits and walk the route carrying buckets to collect money in addition to any sponsorship we could raise. We managed to arrange costumes to be donated to us for the run and managed to rope the area manager of our shop into taking part as well. I was dressed as Little Red Riding hood, and Dave was dressed up as a big friendly dog which went down very well with all the kids at the fun run. One of the men on the team dressed up as Goldilocks which looked particularly amusing as he had a thick full beard and smoked a pipe as we walked the route. We would stop to speak to people in the crowd and ask for money and we even stopped buses in the street and got onboard asking all the passengers to put money in the collection buckets which they all found very funny. Dave looked so great in the dog costume that the local newspaper once again took his photo and reported on the story. We raised enough money to buy the playschool brand new tables and chairs for the children, which was a great feeling. There always seemed to be another worthy cause in need of money so we decided to continue raising funds for more good causes in the local community. Amongst many other events over the years, we organised for many local companies to sponsor us and the school children to complete a fun run wearing T-shirts with the company names printed on them. As Christmas time approached we got the local primary school children involved with sponsored carol singing by the train station to catch people as they came home from work.

Christmas was always the busiest time of the year in the off-licence, with everyone wanting to stock up on drinks for the holiday period. My mother came to visit for the week before Christmas and was able to look after the kids while I worked in the store with Dave. During a quiet moment in the shop she called me in to the lounge to look at something. She told me to look at a certain point on the wall and asked me if I could see a face there. I humoured her by looking and saw nothing. I just laughed and said of course there wasn't anything there. I thought this was very strange and started to worry about her. By this time the shop had filled up with customers again and I needed to get back to help Dave. Due to the hectic nature of the holiday period I put it to the back of my mind and didn't think on the matter again. Finally Christmas day came and we were able to close up the shop and spend time together as a family. After we had finished giving out presents and eating Christmas dinner we were able to sit down and relax in front of the television. I happened to glance at the wall next to the curtains and looking back at me was an image of a man's face. Where one of the eyes should have been there was a cross and there was something criss crossing across the head. I was amazed to see this and realised that this must have been what my mother had seen a week earlier. So I asked her to describe to me what she had seen in detail and it was a perfect description of what I was looking at now. I was able to see this face on the wall for some time after this day although I was never worried by this. Eventually the day came when we needed to redecorate and sadly after this the face was gone. All that was left was the small cross that always remained, which felt very comforting.

Dave and I decided to take the children to Newcastle so that we could all attend my cousin's wedding, and we could spend some time with my family there as a holiday as well. Dave was driving the car on the motorway and the children were fast asleep in the back seat of the car. In the car I used to have a small mirror in front of me on the sun visor and something made me look up at it and I saw a lorry travelling at breakneck speed directly behind us. It looked out of control and was grinding against the metal barrier on the side of the lane and was about to crash into the back of our car. I turned and looked at the children and in my mind I called out 'God help me. The boys are going to die. Help them'. As I thought this Dave turned the steering wheel and we were in the next lane. Another second and the lorry would have ploughed into the back of the car. The lorry sped past us its brakes screeching and eventually hit the car that was in front of us. Thankfully as the car that was in front of us was quite a way ahead the lorry driver had time to brake and reduce his speed before the impact and the people in the car were not badly injured. Although if it had hit us I know the situation would have been much worse. I said to Dave "your quick reactions saved our lives". He replied that he never even saw the lorry behind us and didn't know anything about it. He was just concentrating on the road ahead. I said, "How on earth did you know to move across when you did? It was split second timing." Dave just said that he saw a space appear in the busy lane next to us and moved out. I believe that God and the angels helped us and saved our lives. I asked for help and it was given. How did that space just appear and Dave moved into it at the precise moment without even realising what was about to happen to us? All the cars slowed right down after the impact to make sure the people in the crash weren't hurt and several other drivers called out to us asking how did we manage to get out of that situation.

It was announced that a large Tesco store was going to be built in the area. Dave expressed his concerns to the area manager that if the Tesco was built all of the local shops including ours would lose their customers and end up being forced to close down. The area manager laughed this off suggesting that if anything it would bring more people to the area and we would be busier than ever. Dave was not convinced and sadly he was proved right. More and more supermarkets were built and soon enough all of the local off-licences were closing down until eventually it happened to us too. After twenty-three years of working for the same company they were now selling all of their stores and we were now out of work and without a home. Thankfully the company offered us a redundancy package and although some people may think we were crazy we decided to use some of the money to buy a new car and take the children to Disneyland in Florida. All of our holidays for recent years had been to stay with Dave's mum who was now living in Devon. We felt that we had worked very hard for many years and it was about time we treated ourselves a bit. Dave's Aunt had recently passed away and she had left us some money and the bungalow in Devon, where Dave's mother lived, in the will. When we returned from holiday it was soon time to move out so we rented a house in Rush Green while we looked for a property to buy. We eventually bought a house on Stanley Road South in Rainham, we had decided in advance to stay in the area as the children had lived almost their entire lives in Rainham and we knew it would be very hard for them to lose all the friends that they had made over the years. Despite twenty-three years of experience working in off-licences Dave was now considered too old to be taken on in a similar role and as a result was forced to look elsewhere for work. Dave took a door to door sales job at a double glazing firm to make sure we had some money coming in, although the wages really weren't very good. Dave had been diagnosed as having type 2 diabetes a few years before, which he controlled with medication. His condition had steadily been getting worse, particularly affecting his legs and feet. He was starting to experience neuropathy in his feet, which amongst over symptoms included a numbing sensation almost like pins and needles and a general loss of feeling.

Eventually Dave left the sales job as he didn't enjoy it and there just wasn't enough money in it to support the family. He managed to find a job as a security guard and I took a job working in a gift card and silverware store. On the 31st of August 1997, Dave came home from a night shift in the early hours of the morning and told me that Lady Diana and Dodi Fayed had been killed in a car crash. Like the rest of the nation I couldn't believe what had happened. That morning I travelled to work on the bus and it was absolutely silent, which created a very sad and creepy atmosphere. Everyone looked as though they were in a state of shock. On the journey home quiet music was played on the buses which was continued throughout the week. Shortly after this Dave had been asked to join the security team at Althorp Estate where Lady Diana's body was laid to rest. It was his job to guard the Island in the middle of the lake where Lady Diana was buried. Part of Dave's duty was to guard the gates of the estate. There were thousands of visitors at the estate many leaving bouquets of flowers, in the end the public were asked to stop bringing flowers as the volume of people and flowers had grown so great in the surrounding area that it had become a threat to public safety. Initially Dave would drive around the island throughout the night but Earl Spencer told Dave that the vehicles were disturbing him at night, so instead he would walk for miles around the island every night. When things had calmed down at Althorp Estate Dave came home, however due to all the walking he had developed a large blister on his big toe. As a diabetic, foot care is particularly important and unfortunately Dave's blister had become infected which eventually turned into an ulcer. This turned into a very serious injury and sadly resulted in Dave having to have his big toe amputated and eventually as a result lost his job as a security guard. With hardly any money coming into the house we could no longer make the mortgage payments and it became clear that the only way to resolve this situation and avoid any legal complications was to sell the house. At this time Barry was away studying for his degree at Durham University and I was glad that at least he wasn't at home throughout the worst of our money problems. I remember his first day when he started at the University, Dave and I had driven Barry all the way up to Durham from Essex. After we had helped Barry to unpack all his belongings it was time for us to head home and leave Barry. I held back the tears as I said goodbye to him so as not to upset him. I walked away crying and continued to cry for the seven hour car journey home and most of the following week. He was my youngest and now he was living on the opposite side of the country.

Our financial situation was now very bad and the only way forwards was to sell our house. We were extremely fortunate to have been left the house in Devon in a will and we discussed our house and the house in Devon we would have enough money to buy a house outright that would be big enough for us all to live in. The only problem was that Dave's mum would only agree to this if we moved away from London. We had no real option so we agreed to this and we also liked the idea of living somewhere with some countryside. In the end the three of us decided to move to Weston-super-Mare in Somerset. This broke my heart as my eldest son Taro did not want to leave London and did not have time to find a new place to live by the time the move came around. Thankfully he was able to stay with a friend who was living with his parents and eventually they got a flat in London together. We visited Taro regularly but I always felt sad at the way we had to leave before he was settled somewhere new. Our new home was a lovely large house with four bedrooms and two bathrooms and a double garage. Our next door neighbour was a builder and he agreed to convert the garage, downstairs cloak room and the utility room into an annex so that Dave's mum would have her own space to live. We also had a conservatory built on to the back for her so it ended up being a lovely place for her to live, with me and Dave in the connected house next door. We moved into our new home on 09/09/1999, which seemed like quite a coincidence. I believe that seeing patterns in numbers can be a positive sign and that all numbers have a meaning. Strangely enough we had moved into house number 17, which was the same house number that Barry had just moved into in Durham, and also Taro soon after moved into number 17 in London and my mother had just moved into number 17 in an area of sheltered housing in Essex. We had all moved around the same time and all ended up living at number 17. I felt that this was perhaps too significant for it to be just a coincidence. I looked in to the meaning of the number 17 in Doreen Virtue (PhD) and Lynette Brown's book 'Angel Numbers' which states "You're on the right path with your thoughts. You have good reason to feel optimistic about your plans and path. This powerful and sacred number also represents the holy Trinity and the pyramids". I found this to be a very reassuring message and definitely a positive sign about our future.

Shortly after moving we got a new dog, a Golden Retriever puppy called Merlin. He was adorable and has such a pretty face, people have always stopped in the street to make a fuss of him. Merlin was quite a handful as a youngster and was a little bit naughty. He loved chewing up the furniture and whenever he saw another dog he was completely uncontrollable. At the age of 17 months we decided to take Merlin for some obedience training, however the trainer told us that he was completely untrainable. However we persevered and trained him on our own and Merlin turned out to be an extremely loyal and faithful friend. He has always been a very good and well behaved dog. I think that this just goes to show that you should never give up on something or someone just because a person tells you it is hopeless. You should always trust your intuition and believe your own truth.

We settled in and life continued as normal for a time. Until one morning I sat up in bed and looked over at Dave's foot which was lying on top of the bed covers and saw that it had a white aura all around it including around the area where the big toe had been amputated. I could see the big toe clearly although it was completely transparent, almost spirit like. I found this fascinating and I was really pleased to have seen it. I explained what I had seen to Dave and he said you can understand why some people experience the sensation of a limb long after it has been removed. Some people rationalise this by saying it is related to irritation or inflammation in severed nerve endings sending false messages to the brain. Although I believe that the spirit limb is still present after an amputation, as I saw with Dave's big toe. I experienced something similar one day when I suddenly woke up in the early hours of the morning. I reached over to the bed side cabinet to pick up my glass of water but when I looked across it was not my arm that was reaching over for the glass. It looked whitish and transparent. I believe that it was in fact my spirit arm that I was controlling as my real arms were still by my side. I believe that as I had woken with a start and had not returned properly to my body. This I believe is known as the astral body. I believe that as humans we are all beings of light and energy and that we exist both in our spiritual and physical bodies.

On another occasion I woke up in the night to see a young boy looking back at me. Only the top half of his body was there. Below the waist there was nothing. He was wearing a very old fashioned shirt with a large white collar that reminded me of an old Thomas Gainsborough painting. He moved towards me to get a closer look and then slowly shook his head from side to side as if saying no. I believe he was looking for someone and was expecting to see them lying in the bed. He looked at me as if to say that he didn't recognise me and couldn't understand why I was there. I wasn't frightened by this experience perhaps because I was now used to seeing apparitions and other such unusual things, or because on some level I knew that there was nothing for me to fear. I got the strong impression that angels were guiding him towards the light, although I can't really explain how or why this information came to me. The boy began to float higher and higher within the room and as he rose sparks of light, like a trail of stars, glittered around his body. I believe that this light was in fact energy sparks signifying that angels were present. He stopped as he reached a large picture of my two sons taken when they were both very young that I kept hung on the wall in the bedroom. After looking at the picture for a while he continued to rise up and travelled through the ceiling until he had completely disappeared from the room. I believe he was searching for something and I hope the angels were able to guide him to where he needed to be.

These strange visions usually come to me at night or first thing in the morning and I believe that other people who witness such things have also reported this. I think that this is because we are at our most relaxed at this time and therefore at our most open minded. Also at night things are quiet and there are no other distractions demanding your attention. Another night I looked over to Dave while he slept and his whole head was covered in a white aura and there was a white/grey trail of smoke coming from his mouth going upwards as he breathed out. It flowed in and out of his mouth as he breathed and it was fascinating to watch. I believe that I was seeing Dave's spiritual energy. Some time later I had my aura read by an expert and while I was there I explained what I had seen to her and she said it sounded like I had seen ectoplasm, although I have only ever heard of ectoplasm in regard to mediums and spirits. Sometimes when you are seeing things that cannot be explained by rational tangible means it can be difficult to fully explain what you have experienced, as you feel as if there aren't words to express what you have felt and seen.

Cosmic Energy

Through a portal an energy flowed,
Cosmic energy shimmered and glowed.
Cascading down like a waterfall,
Vibrating to a sound, a call.

Bathing you in a golden ray,
Giving a power to every day.
With every breath you take,
Breathing in an energy filled lake.

Flowing through your every cell,
Feeling balanced feeling well.

As images create your present,
Across oceans on a moon lit crescent.
A magical spell was cast,
Of memories of the past.

Just focusing your mind,
Peace and calm you will find.
A universal energy store,
Pulsating within the earth's core.

An unconditional love,
An awareness from above.
Through a portal an energy flowed,
Cosmic energy shimmered and glowed.

Dave was now suffering a great deal with pains in his legs and
feet as a result of his diabetes and neuropathy, and I longed to
find a way to be able to help him. I have always loved reading
and when I was in my local bookstore I felt drawn over to one

particular book. Whenever I was in the book shop I found myself going over to it and picking it up. I felt that maybe this book was meant for me so eventually I bought it. The book provided a basic outline of what healing is and how it works. After reading the book I decided to attempt healing myself. I placed my hands a few inches above Dave's leg where he was getting the most pain and I could feel the energy flow from my hands into Dave. I asked Dave if he had felt anything and he said the experience was amazing, as if the pain was being drawn right out of him. He said it felt like water running through his legs. After this first session Dave would always ask me to place my hands over his legs and feet to heal him. I was glad that I was now able to do something to help ease his pain. Since that first attempt I developed a deep passion for healing and have dedicated many years to honing and developing my skills and trying to help as many people in need as I can. I have completed Certificates 1 & 2 of the N.F.S.H (National Federation of Spiritual Healers), diplomas in Counselling and Chakra Healing, and taken further courses in Meditation and Healing.

When I am about to perform healing on someone I start by sitting them down on a chair and standing behind them. I always take time to ground myself and the person I am healing before I begin. This ties us both to the earth and prevents either of us feeling light headed or weak during the session. I do this by imagining golden roots stemming from the bottom of my feet and flowing deep down to the core of the earth. Then I allow the energy to draw up from the tip of the roots all the way back up to my feet, rising into my ankles, up into my knees, my pelvis, my stomach and then feeling the energy flow all the way up my spine leaving me feeling empowered, focused and with a firm stable foundation. When I have completed this process on myself I would then repeat it for the person who I am healing. Then I attune myself by visualising a white light flowing down from above my head, through my crown chakra, through my body and out through my hands. This process enables the channelling of energy through you so you can heal. In my mind I then ask the higher self of the person that I am about to heal for permission to heal them. I then contact Archangel Michael and ask for protection and I visualise a separate white light of protection around both myself and the person I am about to heal. This whole process only takes about a minute and is easily remembered by the acronym GAPP, which stands for 'Grounding', 'Attuning', 'Permission' and 'Protection'. I then place my hands on the person's shoulders and let the energy flow through them. When I start the actual healing I always work a few inches away from the body as I can feel the energy much stronger this way. It is not necessary to physically touch someone in order to provide healing for them. During the healing process I work to clear and balance the seven main chakras. The idea of chakras originated from Hinduism and the name is derived from the Sanskrit word for wheel. A chakra is a spinning vortex of energy known as chi or prana. The chakras are part of our energy system and look after our mental, physical, emotional and spiritual well being. The chakras control the energy flow throughout the body and if these chakras become unbalanced or blocked it can cause illness or emotional problems. When healing I can feel stronger vibrations where there are energy blocks and I focus on that area until I can feel the blockage is cleared and the energy is flowing smoothly. Each of the seven main chakras relate to different parts of the body but if there is a disturbance it will not only affect the corresponding organs and glands connected to that chakra but can unbalance the whole body. Each of the chakras are associated with and stimulated by its own colour and if that colour appears dirty or dull you can tell that there is a blockage and as a result an illness relating to the connecting part of the body. When the healing is performed and the blockage is removed the colour resonates to a clearer and brighter colour. When all the colours of the chakra are spinning vibrantly and clear then the body has well-being. Not everyone can see these colours but you can still feel whether a chakra is blocked or clear when healing as each chakra vibrates at a frequency drawing universal life force from the earth into our body to bring us balance, harmony and to help to develop our consciousness.

The Root chakra, also referred to as the Base chakra, is situated at the base of the spine and resonates to the colour red. When this chakra is unbalanced it can lead to feelings of insecurity. However when this chakra is balanced it will give you a strong connection to nature and a feeling of being grounded. When the energy is flowing clearly in this chakra it makes you feel more healthy and energised and is also linked to willpower. The Sacral chakra is located just below the navel and resonates to the colour orange. This chakra is affected by our thoughts and feelings and when cleared it allows us to explore our creativity and enjoy the experience of life. The Solar-Plexus chakra is located just above the navel and resonates to the colour yellow. This chakra is linked to the digestive system and the pancreas and when balanced it can help you find your personal power and develop your sense of intuition. The Heart chakra is located in the middle of the chest and resonates to the colour green. When balanced this chakra allows us to love unconditionally without anxiety and distress and gives a feeling of wholeness and of being at one with yourself. The Throat chakra is located in the centre of the throat and resonates to the colour blue. This chakra allows us to express ourselves creatively with feelings and emotions and also relates to our communication skills. This chakra is linked to the neck, throat, mouth, jaw, ears and thyroid. The Third Eye chakra is located between the eyebrows and resonates to the colour indigo. When balanced this chakra allows us to connect to our higher self and our intuition. This chakra is associated with the eyes, nose, pituitary glands and sinuses. The Crown chakra is located at the top of the crown of the head and resonates to the colours violet or white. When balanced this chakra allows us to connect with the universe and a higher level of consciousness and cosmic energies. People whose crown chakra is balanced usually feel at peace with themselves. The crown chakra is linked to the skull and the brain.

Sometimes when people are too ill they cannot get to you regularly for healing, and others just live too far away to make it practical. Whenever any member of my family who doesn't live with me gets ill I always send them distance healing. This is a method used to offer healing to someone when they are not physically near you. In order to do this I start by meditating and then ask Archangel Michael for protection both for myself and the person who I want to send healing energy to. I visualise a white light around myself and imagine seeing the person I want to heal and then visualise a white light around them too. After this I then thank Archangel Michael for the protection. Then I say the words "I call upon Archangel Raphael" three times, and then ask for his healing green energy to be sent through the person receiving healing. Then I visualise sending a healing light from myself to flow all around the person and through every cell of their body and I imagine seeing that person looking healthy, happy and smiling. I then thank Archangel Raphael for his healing energy and say "amen".

In addition to healing, another method that can be used to clear the chakras is meditation. I like to meditate for about twenty minutes every day. I do not use music or chanting, I just sit quietly, try to still my mind and I feel the energy all around me and in every cell of my body. Meditation quietens and focuses the mind from everyday chatter and the turmoil of the world around us. It is very peaceful, calming the mind, reducing stress and bringing a sense of physical relaxation and well-being, allowing you to feel healthier. When I have finished healing or meditating I visualise each chakra closing just a little, so as to keep the chakra balanced and to prevent the chakra from becoming overactive. I then ask Archangel Michael to release any negative energies or entities from me and I ask for his strength, courage, peace and faith to flow through me, and for his protection to surround me.

Below are some guided meditations that I have prepared:

Guided Meditation I

You find yourself in a rich green wood looking up into the top of the trees. As the sun's rays flicker through the branches it sends a warmth through you that fills every cell of your body. Starting in the toes and flowing up your feet into the ankles continuing up into your legs. Into your thighs and the buttocks. Feel all the tension leaving you and your muscles relaxing. The warmth flows up your body, into your stomach. Sending a glowing warmth rising upwards. Building and growing and warm rising to your heart releasing an unconditional love. Flowing up your spine into your shoulders. Deeply relaxing the shoulders and flowing down the arms and into the hands and fingers. Then back up the arms into the neck and the face and head. Every muscle relaxing. Now visualise a white protective light completely covering you and protecting you from harm and negativity. Knowing that now you are in a completely safe place and relaxed, ready to continue your journey.

You take off your shoes and feel the grass on your bare feet and in between your toes. You smile at how peaceful and free that you feel. As you walk along by a clear sparkling stream you can hear the birds singing and smell the delicate fragrance of the flowers. Bluebells cover the area around each tree as well as buttercups and red and white roses. The colours are so bright. You look at a white rose. You smell it and touch it. Each petal feeling soft like velvet. You then wash your hands in the stream and feel all your worries and tension leaving you. Washing away into the stream. You see it changing into beautiful rainbows. Leaving you feeling peaceful and relaxed. With your feet firmly on the grass you visualise golden roots flowing from the soles of your feet into mother earth. Deep, deep down. You now feel grounded protected and safe.

You look up to see a pure white unicorn. His horn spiralling golden energy and his wings of silver mist. He asks you to use the large stepping stones to cross the stream. Each step you take you count as you cross. One. Two. Three. Four. Five. And then your feet sink into the rich green grass and the unicorn asks you to make a wish. He says that one wish will be granted. Take a moment of quiet time to think about what wish you would like to ask the unicorn for. Having given the unicorn your wish he then thanks you for visiting him. You can always return and visit the unicorn again as many times as you want to.

It is now time to continue your journey. The sun's rays flicker through the trees and you look down into the stream which is now sparkling with small rainbows. Green, red, yellow and orange. Many colours dancing in between small pebbles as the water splashes sounding like the tinkling of bells. As you continue your journey the colours of the flowers and the green of the trees look brighter and clearer. You see a large golden glow, as large as a person. As you look at the dazzling golden light an angel appears and smiles at you. He softly and gently takes your hands as you lie down on the grass. He is carrying a white basket full of coloured crystals. He places a ruby red crystal near the base of your spine. The crystal then changes in colour from a dull red to a bright clear red. The angel then places an orange crystal just below your belly button. As the orange crystal clears and brightens you feel the warmth of the crystal on your body. Then the angel places a yellow crystal just above the belly button. As the crystal clears and brightens it glows like the sun. The angel then takes a green crystal from the basket and places it in the centre of your chest. As this crystal clears and brightens it sends unconditional love through you. The angel brings a light blue crystal and places it on your throat. When this crystal clears and brightens it is the colour of the sky and it allows you to speak truthfully. The next crystal is indigo coloured and is placed in the centre of your forehead so that you may have clarity. As this crystal clears and brightens you can now see things more clearly. The angel now places a purple crystal just above your head. All of the crystals are now clear and sparkling and all your energy centres are balanced. You have an intense feeling of well-being. The angel collects all of the crystals, putting them back into the white basket. When you look into the basket the crystals have dissolved into a golden light, leaving just a pen and paper. The angel asks you to take the pen and paper and tells you to write down any worries you have and then place the pen and paper back into the white basket. Take a moment to think about what you want to write. The angel thanks you and tells you that he will take the basket with your worries in it and heal them. If you have any more worries you can call on the angel anytime so that he can heal them. The angel spreads his beautiful wings and floats upwards carrying your basket of worries away and sends down a golden healing light that flows through every cell of your body leaving you feeling relaxed, safe and confident.

As you thank the angel and wave goodbye you walk back across the stepping stones counting each step backwards. Five. Four. Three. Two. One. Now across the stream you make your journey home. Everything is much brighter and clearer now. As you walk along you feel the grass beneath your feet and between your toes. You feel a new found sense of freedom. You feel full of energy but at the same time relaxed and calm. Feeling that whatever the next day may bring you always know that you can call on the angels and the unicorns to face it with you.

Now you visualise those golden roots leaving the soles of your feet and flowing deep, deep into the ground and drawing up the earth's energy into you. You find a soft purple cape lying on the ground. You pick it up and place it around your shoulders, pulling up the hood so you are now completely enveloped in this soft beautiful purple cape that will give you all the protection you need. Now you are feeling refreshed, safe, protected and loved.

Magical Unicorn

The unicorn comes to us in our dreams
That sparkles and gleams
Shielding us from the night
A golden hue
Surrounding you
Connecting over a heavenly dew
A horn of spiral light

White feathers falling through the air
Descending down without a care
Floating on a breeze
Swaying in the trees

Dancing in and out of rainbows
A magical being
A mystery of healing
A wondrous feeling
Guiding us through our dreams
Reflecting across a crystal stream.

Golden energy radiating light
Glimpses forever, just out of sight
Watching over us, from our birth
A harmony of rhythms of the earth

A gift lay dormant
A magical moment
A unicorn in our dreams

Stepping Stones

Through a winding corridor
Stood rows of open doors
Each one opening
As another one is closing
Choices to be made
Before they can fade

Following a path
On your behalf
Foot-steps leaving a print
A memory or a hint

Of the future, of the past
Each thought to last
Like the ticking of a clock
As each key unlocks
The wonders are shown
To explore the unknown

A simple need to grow
To let your energy flow
A need to evolve
Life's lessons to solve

Reaching out together
Knowing life is forever
Silent humming tones
When you cross
The stepping stones

Guided Meditation 2

Take a deep breath in, and hold it for a little while. Then breath out feeling relaxed and knowing that you are in a very safe place. Now tense your toes tightly and then your ankles. Tightening the muscles in your legs and your buttocks. Tightening the muscles in your stomach travelling up into your chest, shoulders and neck. Tensing and tightening the muscles down your arms, into your hands, tightening them into a fist. Feel the tension travel back up your arms into your face. Now all your muscles are tensed take a deep breath in. Hold it for a little while and then as you breath out feel all your muscles relax and all the tension in your body leaving you. You are now feeling completely relaxed and safe. Now I want you to visualise golden roots leaving the soles of your feet, flowing deep, deep down into the earth. Now feel the earth's energy flowing up the roots into your body filling every cell with peace, courage and strength. Now visualise a white light completely enveloping all around you like a warm blanket, knowing that you are in a completely relaxed, peaceful and safe place.

You find yourself standing on a beautiful golden beach as your feet sink into the warm sand. You sit down with your back up against a palm tree feeling the energy from the tree flowing into you. You get up and walk towards the deep blue sea. You walk out to sea until the water is up to your ankles. The water is so clear you look down to see sea urchins and shells both large and small glistening like jewels as the sun reflects across the sea. You pick up a large sea shell and hold it up against your ear, you can hear the waves and a soft singing sound. As you look out into the distance you can see six dolphins swimming towards you and you realise that the singing you heard was actually that of the dolphins. As they swim closer towards you, you can feel the peaceful energy that is flowing from them completely engulfing you like a soft warm blanket. You feel their gentle energy seeping into every cell of your being and you thank the dolphins for sending their energy to you. You pick up the shell from the beach and place it to your ear once again and as the dolphin's swim away you can hear them singing. Walking back to the palm tree you stop when you see what looks like a large white bird in the sky, swooping down and landing near you on the beach. As the large white wings unfold you can see that it is not a bird but a beautiful angel with a golden glowing aura around him. He is reaching out to you and asking you to hold his hand. As you take his hand a mist descends over you. The mist clears to reveal a unicorn whose horn of golden energy glistens in the sun's rays and looks at you with eyes that are full of kindness. As you look into his eyes, that are as blue as the sea, he asks you to take a gift out of the blue velvet pouch that hangs around his neck. Placing your hand in the bag and taking out a gift, you thank the unicorn. The angel speaks and tells you to keep this gift as it has a special meaning just for you, and any time you are feeling troubled or worried it will allow you to feel peaceful and protected.

(I am going to give you a moment now so that you can accept the gift of healing from your unicorn, and if you choose you can ask him his name. You can tell the unicorn anything that is troubling you, and as you do, visualise a golden energy leaving the unicorn's horn and flowing through you. Knowing you are safe and loved).

You thank the unicorn for his gift and healing. You watch as he spreads his majestic wings and floats up into the white clouds until he disappears out of sight. The angel takes your hand and guides you back to the palm tree. You thank the angel and he disappears with a golden glow. You sit down once again with your back against the palm tree, feeling at one with all that surrounds you. You watch the gentle waves ebbing back and forth onto the beach and hear the distant singing of the dolphins. As you glance up at the blue sky the sun's rays beat down and a rainbow appears gently touching you with each colour. Red flows across you giving you a feeling of security. Then the colour orange which brings balance to your thoughts and feelings. Then a yellow as bright and clear as the sun releases all your fears. Then the colour green filling you with a feeling of unconditional love, followed by a light blue that enables you to speak the truth. This is followed by the colour indigo which gives you clarity and allows you to see things more clearly, then changing into the colour purple bringing you peace and knowledge. You look up to the sky and the rainbow fades away leaving you now feeling balanced safe and loved.

Now standing up, visualise those golden roots out of the soles of your feet flowing deep, deep down into the ground. You pick up a velvet cloak that is lying next to you and put it on, pulling up the hood so that it completely covers you, knowing that you are grounded, safe, protected and loved.

Atlantis

Golden Atlantis bathed in light
Energy filled crystals a divine sight
An invisible barrier of love and healing
With crystals and colours forever appealing
Flowing to the rhythm of a heart
An explosion of colours drift apart
A welcoming sound to the power of the mind
Of wisdom and wonder for all to find

In the ocean, lights sparkled
An energy was rekindled
From the planets and the stars
Reaching out as far as mars
Watching as dolphins swim
Protecting everyone without a whim
Spirit of energy
Travelling through space
Thin veils of mist
like golden lace

As the calming music flowed
The energy soothed and glowed
Revealing an innocence
A relaxing, calming oneness

The healing temples
In all its glory
With tales of healing
And a story
A higher vibration, sending messages
To a guru and wise old sages

As Atlantis sank, without a trace
Wisdom and knowledge grew
Throughout the human race
In spirit golden Atlantis rose
Bathed in light
Healing hue of rainbow colours
A divine sight

As part of my training when I was studying for the N.F.S.H certificates I was to perform healing on another member of the group. I performed the healing in my usual way and everything seemed to be going well, when all of a sudden the woman receiving the healing burst in to tears and began sobbing. I became quite worried and wondered what I had done wrong to make her cry like this, but then the woman kept thanking me over and over again. She told me that when she was being healed she could see and feel her baby in her arms. When she had calmed down she explained to me that her baby had died several years ago and that she had never experienced anything like this before in her life. She said that she was so grateful to me for the experience and I felt very pleased for her and glad that I was able to bring some sense of joy and peace to her after such a tragic event. Later that afternoon I was to perform healing on one of the N.F.S.H board members, which made me feel very nervous. During the healing I kept my hands a few inches away from the back of her neck for some time as I felt a strong vibration in that area. After I had finished she told me that while I was giving her healing it felt as if a bone in the back of her neck was moving. I told her that this was because the bone was out of alignment and I was putting it back in place for her. She thanked me for correcting it and told me that my healing energy was clearly very strong.

Not everyone is open minded about healing but I don't believe in wasting energy trying to persuade people that what I do is genuine. I do not have anything to prove and I am here for all the people that want to come to me for healing. However one of the people that had come for a healing session with me admitted that he was a sceptic and didn't think it would work, but was prepared to give it a try. He had been experiencing a lot of pain in his shoulder and had been receiving treatment from the doctor for a very long time, but he still could not raise his arm very far in the air without it causing him terrible pain. He felt that he had tried everything and nothing seemed to work and that was what had led him to my door, so I gave him a full healing session. I felt a strong pulsating vibration beneath my hands when I placed them over his shoulder, I always feel the vibration strongest where the problem is, and the energy moving and the blockage slowly clearing. When I had finished healing him, he stood up and raised his arm high up in the air and said he was amazed that it felt so much better. He was sorry for doubting my abilities and he became a regular client coming to see me every week for more healing and in exchange he would cut the grass in the front garden every week when he came over.

One day I noticed that my gums felt very sore and swollen. There was clearly something wrong so I went to the dentist, who told me that I had a gum infection around a tooth that had been capped. He said that the tooth needed to come out but there was no way that he would be able to do it himself, as when I had the tooth capped it was screwed in to the root and it had set really strongly. He explained that the only option was to go to hospital to have the tooth removed. I did not like the idea of having to go to the hospital for this and it made me very worried. That night I placed my hand over the problem tooth and I could feel the energy flowing through it which created a 'fizzing' sensation. In the morning I was surprised to find that a hairline crack had appeared all the way around the centre of the tooth. So that morning I went back to the dentist who was shocked to see that the crack had appeared in the tooth and couldn't understand how it could have happened overnight when there had been no sign of it the previous day. As a result he was able to remove the tooth easily himself and I didn't need to go to the hospital after all, which was a great relief.

We invited my mother to stay for a week's holiday and she had a lovely time with us in Weston-super-Mare. So much so, that she told us that she wished she didn't have to leave at the end of it. Dave suggested to me that we invite my mother to live with us. We already had his mother living next door in the annex and it would be nice if she came to live with us too. My mother was delighted at the news and after several weeks of making arrangements she left her home in sheltered housing in Grays, Essex and joined us in Weston-super-Mare. It was lovely to have my mother living with us again, as she had done for a time in Rainham.

I believe that the angels are never far away and they are just waiting to help us but they can only help if we ask them to. I also believe that they try to communicate with us but not everyone understands how to listen to them or how to read the signs. When I went away on a healing course we were told to ask the angels for a white feather to come to us as a sign that they were watching over you. The following morning when I was back at home I asked the angels for a white feather to come to me and decided to go out for a walk. As I stepped out into the driveway just a few steps from my doorstep I saw a white feather right in front of my feet. Angels will often send white feathers to people to let them know that they are not alone and that they are following the right path. My son Barry has also had some unusual experiences regarding angel signs in the form of receiving white feathers. Ever since Barry was a little boy he had a gift for music, but at age 16 he gave up A-Level music after only one class saying that it was really designed for classical music students, which wasn't the sort of music he was interested in. Barry lost touch with his interest in music and focused on more academic subjects in his further studies. However at aged 24 Barry, seemingly on a whim, decided to buy a very good synthesiser and rekindled his interest in music. At the time Barry was working in Accountancy for a property management company and working on the 3rd floor. His desk was right by a window which was usually left open as it got very stuffy in the office. Shortly after deciding to buy the synthesiser and get back in to music, Barry saw a white feather fly in through the window, and circled right around his head before landing in his open palm. I believe that this was a very strong sign that his future lay in music not accountancy. Currently at the time of writing Barry is going through a career change so that he can dedicate much more time to music and is also about to start studying Sound Engineering and Music Production at a prestigious music technology college. Just a few days ago while Barry was taking a break from working on this book we were out in town and a white feather dropped right in front of him landing on his chest as we were walking. This was followed by another white feather that dropped next to his foot just a few seconds later. We looked at the sky but there were absolutely no birds in sight. I believe that this is also a powerful sign that we are on the right path by writing this book together. I believe that angels can send us signs in a number of ways ranging from the subtle to the more obvious, or just by planting the seed of an idea in your head. One morning I woke up and the first thing that I saw were the words 'Well-Being' written across the front of my wardrobe in beautiful italic writing. It remained there for a few minutes and then it disappeared. That day the words well- being kept coming in to my mind without me even thinking about it. I think the angels were telling me that I needed to take better care of myself.

Angel Signs

White feathers falling through the air,
Angels showing that they care.
Descending down at your feet,
As your heart skips a beat.
Signs from angels from above,
Sending comfort, guidance and love.

A friction of energy sparkling,
A trail of colours flickering,
Rainbows of angel lights,
Moving fast, out of sight.
Guiding you upon your sacred journey,
With an inner peace and harmony.

As you walk along the beach,
The angels are within our reach,
A sign that they are close to you,
Rainbows and feathers are a clue.

Looking out at a feathery cloud,
Calling to us, clear and loud.
Spanning out across the sky,
With guidance and choices to try.
Sending comfort for all to see,
A warmth, a glow just for me.

There is no pretence,
Just a loving presence.
As the day is dawning,
The birds give their warning.
Of magic, mystery and vision,
Helping us make the right decision.

Realms of spirit, healing and wisdom
Giving insights into our freedom.

A celestial sign, a hidden charm,
Guiding you away from harm.
A harmonious song, a musical tone,
Knowing you are never alone.

Showing you the way,
Each and every day.
Signs from angels from above,
Sending comfort guidance and love.

A friend of Dave from his disabled swimming classes came to me for healing one day. He had an accident many years ago and as a result sustained a serious injury, which required him to have a metal plate put into his back. He also had an old football injury which meant that he felt a lot of pain in his shoulder. He had been retired through disability ever since he injured his back. After I performed healing on him he said that he felt so relaxed and despite me not touching him and his eyes being shut, he always knew what part of his body I was working on because of the intense heat that came from my hands. He visited me for another three healing sessions after which he told me that he had spoken to his doctor and they had agreed to halve his medication as he felt that since coming to me for healing he didn't need it as much. In fact his condition had improved so greatly in the month that he had been coming to see me that he was well enough to go back to work on a part-time basis. I always explain to my clients that they should also go and see a doctor and should never cut down on their pain medication without discussing it with them. I do not have a medical background and would not assume to know better than a doctor on matters such as medication. I believe that what I do is complimentary to whatever medical treatment the client is receiving from their qualified practitioner.

One of my other clients was a man named John. John had recently suffered a heart attack and was not able to walk very far and experienced a lot of pain in his legs when he did walk. After his first two sessions he said that he felt so relaxed and peaceful and his movement felt far less restricted. However during John's third healing session he slumped forwards in his chair, his head in his hands. I asked him if he was alright and he replied that he felt a little faint. Sweat was pouring from his face so I got him a glass of water. I had never experienced a reaction like this in all my time as a healer. I suggested that perhaps he would not want to have healing any more after this, but John wouldn't hear of it. "Oh yes I will" he laughed. "I've never felt so relaxed". He described the healing session that he had just experienced as feeling a strong heat that wasn't like the sun or any other kind of heat. He said it felt as though the heat came from within him while I was giving him healing. He looked at me in a baffled way and said "It is amazing how someone so small could have so much energy". As John left I told him to rest when he arrived home and to call a doctor if he felt ill in any way. John said that he actually felt great now, but he would take it easy when he got home anyway. The next week John had brought his wife Anne with him so that she could experience the healing. Anne was disabled and had a mobility scooter as she could not walk very far. After the healing session Anne and I sat talking for a while and she said that it still felt as if my hands were still healing her feet even though the session had been over for several minutes. I explained to her that she could still be feeling the effects of a healing session for some time afterwards as the healing is still working after the actual session is over. She said that during the session it felt as if all the pain in her legs and feet was being melted away and that she saw the colours purple and yellow as if in rolling clouds. A lot of people tell me that they see or experience things when they are receiving healing and many say that they see colours. I'm not sure exactly why people so often see colours and images but I have wondered whether the colours they are seeing while I heal them are linked to the colours of the chakras. After a few sessions Anne said that she was feeling much better and had a lot more energy. When John came back for his next healing session he confided in me that it would have taken an awful lot to convince Anne to believe in spiritual healing but she had admitted to him that there must be something in it because she felt so much better and was able to walk twice the distance that she could manage before. After another session with Anne she once again told me that she had seen the colours yellow and purple, which looked like smoke flowing into a small hole. She told me that she was thinking of painting what she had felt and seen because she could not find words that could explain the depth of the experience. She also said that it felt as though she was going down into the ground and that her body was dissolving. She said that it felt very strange but that it was not in any way frightening, instead it felt very good and positive. Another client once told me that while I was giving her healing it felt as if her body did not even exist, she felt so relaxed and consumed by a feeling of well-being. In exchange for the healing, John and Anne would bring me flowers from their garden and home grown vegetables, even though I never asked them for anything, but it was nice that they wanted to show their appreciation for what I was doing for them. At a much later date I realised that I would have to charge people for healing, just like people do for any complementary treatment, as I needed to make a living as well. It never really occurred to me to charge people for this because I enjoyed being able to help people and that was all I had wanted to get out of the experience. I wish I were financially well off enough to continue to let people receive healing for free.

Usually I give healing at my home but sometimes I have performed healing in unusual places. One day Dave and I were out walking our golden retriever Merlin and I noticed a dog limping. I stopped and asked the owner what was wrong with him and she said that he had been having treatment at the vets but they didn't think there was anything they could do to help him and he would probably have to have part of his leg amputated. I explained that I was a healer and asked if I could try giving him some healing. So in the middle of the park I gave the dog a full healing session focusing particularly on his troubled leg. Once I had finished the dog started jumping around like a spring lamb. I asked if he normally behaved like this and they told me that he usually struggled just to walk let alone jump around like this. Sadly as neither myself or the owner had a pen we were not able to exchange details to enable me to continue healing the dog. It was at this time that I realised that I would need to get business cards made up and carry them around with me to ensure that I can help as many people as possible. There is no reason why healing cannot be performed on animals or in fact any living thing. When I place my hands over a plant I can feel the energy vibrations flowing through them and I have often performed healing on sickly looking plants to help them to recover and grow. On another occasion I was in a jewellery store having my watch strap replaced as it had broken earlier that day and the woman that served me told me that she had a very painful shoulder. I explained to her that I was a healer and she asked me if I could perform healing on her there and then because she was in so much pain. Someone fetched a chair for her to sit on and I performed healing on her right in the middle of the store. You never know when you might meet someone that needs healing and I never like to say no to someone if I think that I can help them.

On 27th June 2004 Taro and his long term girlfriend Teenie were married. Teenie is a lovely girl with olive skin and big brown eyes. She is originally from Sao Paulo in Brazil but had been living in London for several years. Taro and her met while they were both working for the BBC in London. The night before the wedding Teenie and her sister Becky had been patiently waiting for news of their parents arriving in London for the wedding. The phone rang with the sad news that despite their best efforts they could not attend the big day. Circumstances beyond their control had prevented them from being able to make it. Teenie was very upset and disappointed but there was nothing that could be done now. Taro abandoned the traditional idea of spending the night apart from the bride the night before the wedding and not seeing her until the actual wedding on the day itself, so that he could be with her and support her while she was upset. The day of the wedding came and we travelled to Pembroke Lodge in Richmond park for the ceremony, they could not have picked a more beautiful setting for their wedding. Taro and Teenie had worked so hard preparing the hall and making all the arrangements themselves. Taro wore a cream suit and Teenie looked beautiful in her white dress. I thought they looked like a prince and princess. We all felt so proud of them. At the reception Dave read out a speech that Teenie's dad had written, which was a very emotional moment, knowing that he wasn't able to attend the day.

One day Dave and I attended a healing weekend with the late Bill Harrison, who was a well known local faith healer, in Cheddar. There were many workshops and stalls and while I was there I felt very drawn to a book about psychic protection. I had my aura read and one of the first things that the woman reading my aura said was that I should get a book on protecting myself, which was quite a coincidence. Auras are electro-magnetic vibrations of energy which can be seen in the form of colours that can denote personality traits. All living objects are made up of these vibrations and as a result have an aura. Looking at my aura photo she told me that I had a high spirit guide and the magenta colour on my left side signified the protection that the spirit guide was giving to me. The gold on my throat meant that I was good at counselling and the white and gold running down one side meant that in a previous life I was a healer. She told me that as a healer I had definitely earned my stripes. You can teach yourself to see people's auras which is something that I became interested in after having my aura read. To read someone's aura, rather than looking directly at the person I concentrate on looking to one side of them, preferably with a plain light background behind them. I find that by putting the tips of my first fingers and my thumbs together to form a triangle shape Δ and looking through this and then slowly parting my hands I can see the person's aura better. After a while you can begin to see a white glow around the person's head and then with time and practice you may be able to see colours appear. The aura appears around the body but only for a brief moment. The ability to read auras improves with practice so don't lose heart if it doesn't work straight away, although not everyone can see auras. The aura colours are typically linked with the following personality traits:

Green	- empathy, sensitivity, growth, inner strength, healing, balance, trustworthy.
Orange	- creative, original thinking, intelligence, vitality, open, friendly.
Pink	- tender, intuition, caring, romantic, strong sense of morals, calming.
Blue/Aquamarine	- communication, intuition, listening, compassionate, teacher, helpful.
Red	- purposeful, passionate, physical energy, strength.
Yellow	- analytical, intelligent, joyful, creative, decisive, playful, sense of humour.
Purple	- psychic ability, spiritual, imaginative, wise, sensitive, visionary.
Gold	- spiritual, integrity, counselling, wise.
White	- spiritual, godly, divine, inspirational, honest, major life questions answered.

Dave's health issues had now become so problematic that he was now attending weekly visits to both the doctor and the hospital to monitor his situation. He was now having regular checkups for his eyes, kidneys, heart and feet, all stemming from his diabetes. Of primary concern at this time was his foot, which had become very swollen. The doctor took an x-ray and told us that he suspected Dave had the onset of Charcot foot. This is a form of degenerative arthritis which results in the disintegration of the muscles that support the joints in the foot. On top of Dave's numerous health problems he really didn't want to have this as well. A deeper x-ray would be needed the following week to confirm the condition and see if the bone had been infected, but everything so far indicated that Dave did in fact have Charcot foot. I now started to heal Dave's feet every single day, focusing my energy in an attempt to help the situation. He said that it made his feet tingle and took the pain away, and also said it helped the neuropathy in his legs which enabled him to sleep better at night as a result. When we went back for the next x-ray the doctor and the nurse were shocked when they saw his foot because there had been such a great improvement in his feet. The doctor already knew that I was a healer and asked me if I had been doing a lot of healing on Dave's feet recently. I confirmed that I had, and he told me to keep doing whatever I had been doing because it was clearly working. The doctor also took my business card as he had a bad back and told me he would give me a call for healing if it flared up again. It was nice to see that the doctor was so supportive of spiritual healing as sometimes people with a scientific or medical background can be quite dismissive of things that they cannot prove. It just goes to show that spiritual healing can be used in conjunction with medical treatment in order to help people.

Dave developed many problems with his feet as a result of his diabetes. It seemed that no sooner had one problem been resolved, a new problem was developing. Dave was due to have a scan of his foot at the hospital to see if it was infected. I asked the nurse if they could also perform an x-ray of the big toe on his other foot as well as I had sensed a problem in that area when performing healing on him. The nurse dismissed what I had said and condescendingly pointed out that they can't just perform scans because I 'think' there is something wrong. I protested by saying what if I was right and she didn't scan it. Eventually she gave in and performed the scan but making it very clear that she was only doing it to humour me and keep me quiet. When the results of the x-ray came back it was revealed that Dave had a fractured toe which they would not have known about if I hadn't insisted on the extra scan. Although it was not good news I at least felt pleased with myself for sticking to my guns and finding out what the problem was, so that Dave could get the appropriate treatment.

On one of our many visits to the doctor's surgery, the sister was treating an ulcer on the bottom of Dave's foot. She was a very nice lady and knew that I regularly performed healing on Dave. I said the strange thing when I performed healing on his feet lately was that I felt the vibrations much more strongly on the top of his foot, rather than on the bottom where the ulcer was. It felt as if there was a problem in that area of the foot but the doctor and the sister could not find anything wrong when they examined it. A few weeks later Dave developed a problem on the top of his foot exactly where I had felt the vibrations. I could feel the blockage of energy in that area and I must have sensed the imbalance before any physical symptoms revealed themselves.

Over the years I have performed healing on Dave's feet many times, often focusing on the area where his big toe used to be. The other toes on that foot also needed particular attention during healing as they had become very crooked due to the additional pressure put on them for balance. One day during healing Dave said that he could see himself relaxing by a lake with a fishing rod (Dave always loved fishing). He could see himself catching a fish and then pulling hard on the rod, and at the same time it felt as if the line was attached to his toes that were crooked. As he pulled the rod his toes felt as if they were being tugged, stretched and pulled upwards as if straightening.

Times of Change

A new awareness, a time of change
A life for living, a time to rearrange
So much energy, so much sorrow
A world that's full of hope for tomorrow

Focus the anger in a positive way
Heal the earth each and every day
Release the toxins of the past
Bringing a new life, that's to last

Unto you a breath I take
Eyes open wide awake
A new life is born
No one sad or forlorn
Where does all the anger go
Heal the earth and let it show

Visualise a river flow
Cleansing, warming, and tingling
An inner peace of love and healing
Sparkling droplets touching everyone

A world full of laughter and fun
Warming the earth beneath the sun
With an energy flowing, strong but calm
Caressing the river, an open palm

Rainbows flowing across your hand
Disappearing like grains of sand
So much energy left to decay
Focus it in a positive way

Let the anger dissolve
Let the earth revolve
It's part of life's divine plan
For every woman and man
A new awareness, a time of change
A life for living, a time to rearrange

My mother-in-law was moving a piece of furniture in the annexe next door and accidentally knocked it over onto her ankle. She has always been so independent and would prefer to do something herself rather than ask someone for help. She said that she felt a very strong pain in her ankle but when I placed my hands over her it completely disappeared. While I was performing healing her face became very hot and sweaty even though it was a cold day, and then she felt a cold breeze blow across the back of her neck and she saw many different colours flashing before her eyes. When I perform healing I am always at least two inches away from actually touching the person I am healing, yet my mother-in-law said it felt as if her ankle was being held the whole time and manipulated as if by a masseuse. I have also had several other clients say to me that they felt as if I was massaging them during healing sessions when in fact I had not placed my hands on them at all and I was just sending healing energy through them with my hands several inches above their body. Another client said to me that when I healed her it felt like waves running down her back and that it felt as if my hands were on her feet throughout the whole session. In reality I had only worked on her feet for a short while but it quite often happens that when you are working on one part of the body the client feels as if you are somewhere else. Another client who I was healing described the feeling of being healed as though something inside her was being released and that she felt completely relaxed. Like many other people I heal she described seeing lots of white lights before her eyes like an explosion of fireworks. Another client called Peter had a serious accident when he was 21, fracturing the lower part of his spine, which left him paralysed from the waist down. He has been in a wheelchair ever since then and he was now in his fifties. He had no feeling at all in his legs since the accident but when I gave him healing his left foot would move. I didn't mention it at first as I thought it was perhaps an involuntary spasm, but he later told me that he was completely unable to move his legs and yet when I perform healing on him his legs and feet would jump up in the air. The moment I stopped healing, the movement would stop as well.

One day a new client called Wendy phoned me to make an appointment. She had an aggressive form of cancer in a lump on her leg and was receiving chemotherapy and radiotherapy. She arrived at my house on a Thursday afternoon having had a chemotherapy treatment earlier that day. She looked very tired and told me that her head hurt. As she took off her woollen hat she told me how worried she was about how dry her hair had become after the treatment and feared that it might make it all fall out. Wendy was an attractive woman and you could tell that she made an effort to look good. I gave her a full body healing and worked on clearing her chakras and then spent some time focusing on the lump on her leg. Once I had finished she asked me to place my hands over her head once again as it had stopped it from hurting. I agreed to continue providing healing to Wendy throughout her treatments. As she left that day she hugged me and asked how much I charged for the healing. I told her that I would treat her for free throughout the whole process, as I hate to charge people that are seriously ill. I just told her to buy me a candle or something small like that when her chemotherapy was over. Wendy became a regular client who I saw every week and I would regularly send her distance healing as well. She always said that the healing made her feel very relaxed and that while being healed she would see the colours purple and gold. She said that while I was healing her she felt an intense heat and a strong tingling sensation on her leg. The second time that Wendy came to see me the lump looked smaller than before and continued to get smaller after each healing session. The doctors were stunned at how quickly the lump on her leg had decreased in size as it was completely unexpected. The lump had now become small enough for the doctor to perform an operation to remove it. I gave Wendy more healing before she had her operation and wished her good luck. She had been so strong and positive throughout the treatment I really hoped that this would be the end of this painful period in her life and that she could move on to happier times ahead. After the operation Wendy came to visit me at my home. I was delighted to see her looking so happy and well. She could barely contain her excitement as she explained to me that the lump had been successfully removed and that the cancer had been completely cleared from her body. I was overjoyed to hear this. Her long battle was over and she was now in remission. As Wendy left she hugged me tightly and said "thank you for saving my life". I replied that I was just glad to be able to help. I think helping Wendy would have to be my biggest accomplishment and my proudest moment as a healer. After all of our previous healing sessions Wendy and I would sit and talk for some time before she left and we learned a lot about each other's lives. I told her all about the children's story book that I had published in 1997 and how I would love to make a CD recording of the stories contained within it and be able to release it and give some of the proceeds to a children's charity. Unbeknownst to me Wendy still had some contacts from her days working for the BBC in Bristol and had booked a recording studio for me to record my CD and arranged for the people at the studio to donate their time for free. I was so happy to have the opportunity to do this and really enjoyed the experience of reading out my stories and having them recorded. I still have the CD at home and I would love to be able to release this one day and hopefully do something to aid a good cause.

A New Dimension

Leaping into the future
Each loving look to capture
In a world of innocence
Relaxed and never tense
Moving into a new dimension
Clearing all your emotions
With healing and meditation

While balancing the mind
Peace and calm you will find
An awareness of inner-peace
A clarity a gentle release
Clearing all your fears
A symbol through the years

Where the walls are trees
Filled with butterflies and bees
The roof is the sky
Where birds can fly
Carpets are made of grass
Rainbows sparkling like chards of glass

Looking through the windows of the soul
Each acting out a role
Watching as swans float
On an energy filled moat
As the moon's smiling face
Is covered in a cloudy lace

A chandelier of stars
Reaching out to mars
A watery reflection

Bringing about a connection
Into a new dimension

Anne came for her usual healing session and I began by
grounding us both as usual. However when I asked Archangel
Michael for protection I felt a harsh shiver running through my
body and a tingling sensation from head to toe. I felt startled as

this had never happened to me before, but I continued with the session which then proceeded as normal. That night as I closed my eyes to go to sleep I saw pulsating white lights like fireworks flashing before me. I also saw a funnel shaped chakra which looked like some kind of energy centre. A partial picture started to emerge from the right hand side of my vision. I opened my eyes and rubbed them to try and clear this image and the fragmented pictures in my mind disappeared. The following morning I walked to the post office with my mother, who was 90 years old at the time, to collect her pension. We walked along the path lined with high trees and not many houses. All of a sudden we both heard an ear splitting shriek. We looked up at a tree and there was a bird giving a very loud and unusual call. Neither of us had ever heard a bird make such a strange noise before or be as loud as this one. We arrived at the post office and collected my mother's pension and then made our way back home. We took the same route back home and once again heard the same piercing call from the bird, although now it was coming from a side path we were approaching. Suddenly a man appeared from this side path and snatched my handbag from me. He turned and ran back the way that the bird had been calling from. Thankfully there was nothing of value in my bag and I didn't have much money in my purse, but it was a terrible shock to me and my mother all the same. It was a relief that my mother's bag was not taken as well as she had just collected her pension money. I contacted the police and learned that there had been three other similar cases in the area all within a few days of each other. Although the other incidents had been more violent in nature and the man had put a knife to the throats of the women who's bags he had taken. In hindsight I felt very lucky indeed that this had not happened to me. I attended a police line up to try and pick out the man who had stolen my bag but several months had passed since then and I had no idea if the man was in the line up or not. I believe that I had been given several warnings that something bad was going to happen, but I didn't understand the warnings at the time.

On the 14th April 2005 I looked in to my crystal ball and as I gazed in to it I saw a person lying in bed with many people standing around the bed. This image didn't mean anything to me at the time as I didn't know anyone who was ill in bed. Three days later Dave and I were woken up during the night with repeated banging noises on our upstairs bedroom window. Opening the curtains revealed many seagulls all banging in to the window with their beaks. We couldn't believe what we were seeing. We had never experienced anything like this before or since then, it was almost like a scene from Hitchcock's 'The Birds'. After the shock of being woken up by the loud banging I couldn't get back to sleep so I decided to get up and go downstairs and have some breakfast. I placed a piece of bread in the toaster and at the precise moment that I pressed down the lever I heard an almighty explosion that came from outside and all the lights went out. I had no idea what the noise was, or how it had happened. Was it just a coincidence or had I somehow caused this? I eventually found out that the noise had come from the electric mast opposite our house. The repair man told us that the wires on the mast had burned out causing the loud bang, and the electrics were back on after about thirty minutes. About two hours later the phone rang, telling me that my brother Ricky had died. Family members in the area had stayed around the bed all night. Breaking the news to my mother who was living with us was one of the hardest things that I have ever had to do, she was devastated. What I had seen in the crystal ball, the seagulls banging on my window and the electric mast burning out may all have been coincidences. But I have never been someone who believes in coincidences. I believe that everything happens for a reason. I may not be seeing the man with the long white robe anymore but I was still receiving messages and warnings in other forms when something bad was going to happen.

Time and Space

Gentle whispers through the trees
Of feathers floating on a breeze
Messages from a being
A fragrance and a feeling
Of healing and well-being

A divine light of eternity
A tingling warmth of energy
Lifting through thin veils of time
From the source of love
Swooping down from above
A peaceful white dove

Embers flickering from a flame
Knowing life is not a game
Still the mind
And you will find
Courage, hopes and dreams

Freedom from your tears and fears
A sacred journey through the years
An awareness that's awoken
Realms of gifts, a peaceful token
A clarity, clear and open

A galaxy of stars
Illuminating from afar
A vision from the universe
A symbol, a sign
A harmony of song and verse

I believe that birds convey messages to us and I have experienced the warnings from birds both when my handbag was stolen and when my brother sadly passed away. Birds send help and warnings to us in many ways but we do not always know how to notice the signs and apply them to our life. I believe that birds give us wisdom and guidance. In a relaxed state but not asleep an image came to me one night of a white house with an eagle and an owl outside it. The image felt very positive to me. I believe that the birds bring to us messages from the angels. When sitting quietly meditating you can call for help from any bird that represents the type of help that you need. Visualise the bird that you want help from and ask for guidance from them to help with your situation. You can see the birds in your relaxed state and they will come to you with a message. For example an eagle may represent strength or an owl may represent wisdom. To understand the messages sent to you from the birds you must rely on your intuition and the first thoughts and feelings that come to your mind.

One night as I lay in bed with my eyes closed I saw a swirling purple smoke in my mind's eye. When the smoke cleared I could see the sky and then I was looking out to sea. On the sea there were several men wearing yellow life jackets sat in a rescue boat. Although instead of a typical motorised rescue boat this was just a simple rowing boat. On their life jackets were the letter E and F in large black print. After this the image faded and eventually I went to sleep. In the morning I woke up but still with my eyes closed I saw the purple smoke again. After this cleared I saw pages of writing but it was blurred and I couldn't read any of it. I then saw the rescue boat again although this time it was empty and surrounded by wreckage and broken pipes in the sea. The next thing I knew I was sinking below the waves to the bottom of the dark murky sea. It was at this point that the picture disappeared. I had no idea why I was seeing these images or what I could do about them. The thought crossed my mind that the F stood for ferry but I had nothing really to base this on. I told my family and friends about this vision but nobody could offer any advice as to what it could mean. Several months passed by and I had all but forgotten about what I had seen. Then I saw on a BBC news report on the television that an Egyptian Ferry carrying over 1400 passengers had sunk in the red sea. Over 1000 people had died as the 'as-Salam Boccaccio '98' sank about eighty kilometres from the Egyptian coast. While the cause of the accident was not established many of the survivors reported seeing a large fire on board before the ship sank and several people saw thick smoke bellowing out from the engine rooms. There was footage on the news report of men in yellow life jackets sat in life boats and Egyptian frigates on search and rescue missions.

A Child's Cry

Through the thickly twirling mist
Revealing a boy with a hard clenched fist
A voice echoed out, that sounded strangled
Whose hair was matted, knotted and mangled
With hardened stare, and a look of hunger
A drawn gaunt face, a look of wonder

Underweight and unprotected
Left alone and neglected
No pity, No anger, as tears unfold
Of stories of hunger that are untold
Through the thickly twirling mist
was a call
A frame so lean, so small
A forgotten world, a forgotten child
An untold future, for one so mild

My son Barry called down the stairs to me that both the lamps in my and Dave's bedroom had been left on. He switched them off for us but later in the day I saw that they were on once again. This happened several times throughout the day, the lamps turning themselves back on after we had turned them off and left the room. Dave said that it could just be a power surge and that it was nothing for me to worry about. That night as I lay in bed with my eyes shut trying to sleep, it felt as if there was a bright light on in the room. I assumed the bedside lamp had turned itself on again so I opened my eyes and reached out to turn it off, only to find the lamp was still off. I was shocked to see a glowing bright light next to me roughly the size of a person. Then within this light a figure appeared before me. I panicked and turned the bedside light on, worried what was happening. As the lamp turned on the glowing light and the figure both disappeared. I wish I had been braver and asked the figure who he was and why he was here, but my initial reaction was to try and make it go away. Something felt very wrong to me. When strange things happen to me it is usually a warning sign that something bad is coming. Two days later was the 7th of July 2005 London bombings. A series of coordinated suicide attacks in London by four terrorists targeting trains and buses during the morning rush hour. My eldest son lives in London and many of our friends still lived in that area. It was a terrifying time for the majority of the country. Fifty two people were senselessly killed in these attacks and over seven hundred people were injured, many severely and permanently, in the worst ever terrorist incident on British soil.

An Illusion of Life

Two figures entwined standing entranced
Across bleached white sands
The sun's rays flickered and danced
A porcelain ground smooth and white
Breaking up, gone out of sight
A drifting bank of sand
Hovering over hard baked ground
Revealing a shadowy dark mound
Nothing what it really seems
A living world of endless dreams
To drift and float like an ebbing tide
To cross a barrier to the other side

Life is but a nursery to live and to learn
A time that is for living
A time that's for forgiving
A mystifying circle of life
An unbroken band of gold
A new beginning to an end
A future to be told

With nothing what it really seems
A living world of endless dreams
Clasped fingers drifting apart
A solitary figure with broken heart
An Illusion of life

My mother-in-law hadn't been feeling well and after seeing the doctor she went for some tests at the hospital. After many months of seeing different doctors they all confirmed the very sad news that she had a tumour on her liver and there was nothing that they could do to help her. The doctors explained to us that because of the location of the tumour, combined with the fact that she had angina, they would not be able to operate or offer her chemotherapy treatment. She was told that it was definitely terminal cancer and that if she had a biopsy on the tumour it could result in the tumour spreading much faster and dramatically reduce the amount of time she had left. The doctors told her that she would only have a few months to live and that she should focus on trying to enjoy the rest of her life. Throughout this period I performed healing on my mother-in-law every single day particularly focusing my energy on her liver as it helped to relieve any pain and discomfort. My mother-in-law was a very strong person and she insisted that she wanted to get all her affairs in order herself and make all the necessary arrangements, including planning her own funeral. Between us we called all of her family and friends to let them know what was happening. One of the hardest things for her to cope with was that she did not believe she would live long enough to see her first great grandchild be born. Eventually after a few months since hearing the terrible news the doctor arranged for a biopsy to be taken. After all of the arrangements were made my mother-in-law received a phone call from the cancer nurse and told us that there was no trace of cancer in the biopsy that they had taken. We were all amazed and so relieved to hear the good news. It seemed like a miracle as she had been told by several doctors that she definitely had terminal cancer and there was no way to treat her condition. Once we had some time to get used to every-thing that had happened we couldn't understand why so many doctors had confirmed that she was suffering from terminal cancer. I was tempted to confront the doctors and explain how much pain and suffering was caused by their misdiagnosis. How on earth could so many different doctors all have come to the same conclusion? However my mother-in-law believed that she was cancer free purely because of all the healing that I had been giving her every day over a period of several months. The truth is that it is impossible to say whether the doctors were all wrong from the beginning or whether I had helped her body fight the cancer. We were all just very glad that she was healthy and that was all that really mattered to us.

It wasn't very long before my daughter-in-law Teenie went in to labour. The next day Dave and I travelled to the hospital, calling in at the florist for a bouquet of flowers on the way. On the journey we received a call from Taro that that the baby had arrived and that it was a boy. We were delighted at the news and couldn't wait to get to the hospital to meet him. When we arrived we had to wait outside the room as Teenie was having a shower. The next thing we knew a red light was flashing and Taro rushed out calling for a nurse. There was a moment of panic and we felt completely helpless as nurses rushed in to see her. We had no idea what was happening and we were desperately worried. After a few minutes Taro came out of the room and told us we could come in and see Teenie and the baby. She had collapsed in the shower and needed a blood transfusion. She looked so pale and drained. Taro stayed with her in the hospital for the next few days and took care of the baby, as Teenie was too weak. I could feel the love that he was sending them both. Despite all the drama it was wonderful to see my first grandchild, Joshua Kai Russell. He was such a beautiful baby and has grown in to a very handsome little boy. He has his mother's olive skin and big brown eyes.

Over the years living with us, my mother experienced several health problems and she was suffering from dementia. She needed a lot of care, but as I was no longer working and already acting as a carer for Dave, I had the time to give her the help that she needed. One day she wasn't feeling well and had gone to bed in the afternoon. She said her feet were freezing cold so I placed an extra blanked over her. I explained to her that I couldn't put the central heating on as it was actually a warm summer's day and everyone else was feeling too hot as it was. I checked in on her a little later and she told me that she so felt much better since I had put the heating on for her. I thought that she must be mistaken but when I placed my hands on the small radiator by her bed it was very hot. I checked all of the other radiators around the house and they were all cold. I also checked the thermostat and it still showed that the central heating was off. I checked the radiator in my mother's room again and it had started to cool. It had come on long enough to warm my mother in her room without affecting the rest of the house and without anyone actually switching it on. It was the only radiator that had warmed up in the whole house and it had just heated up on its own while switched off. When something completely unexplainable like this happens it is usually the angels lending you a helping hand. It made me feel that the angels were looking after her during her time of illness.

My mother's dementia was becoming steadily worse and she was becoming paranoid that people were trying to hurt her. It got to the point where she could no longer be left alone in the house even for a brief moment and we could no longer cope by ourselves. The doctor's had advised us to find a nursing home for my mother a year prior to this but I didn't have the heart to. I cared for her as long as I could and probably much longer than I should have. Caring for her had become a full time job for me and the only real respite that I got was in the evenings when Barry came home from work. He would get up in the night if she needed any help or if she had got up and was confused, and then get her back to bed. Even though it broke our hearts we found the only nursing home in the area that specialised in caring for patients with dementia. Even though it was terribly sad, she settled in quickly and seemed happy at the home. I visited her three times a week and I asked the angels to be with her to protect her, keeping her happy and peaceful. I would also send her distance healing whenever I meditated. Some other family members didn't agree with our choice of nursing home for my mother but I knew that we had done everything we could to ensure her health and happiness. I also knew that I had done more for her than anyone else and put her needs above my own for a long time. Sadly my brother decided to take my mother to live in a new nursing home in Essex, even though we feared the journey would be too much for her in her fragile state. Her condition had been steadily deteriorating for some time and she had become extremely weak. Nevertheless he drove my mother to Essex on the bank holiday weekend and sadly she passed away the following day. Although we were all desperately upset to say goodbye to her, she had been very ill for some time and was ninety three when she passed away. On the day of the funeral I prayed to the angels for peace so that we could mourn for my mother without any disagreements amongst family members. I asked for the angels to send me the sign of a rainbow so that I knew the day would be free from any kind of hostility, although in the days preceding the funeral there had been no sign, which left me feeling worried. However the funeral passed by in a peaceful manner and we were all able to pay our respects to my mother, who was a wonderful woman and was very much loved by many people. On our drive home Barry called out to me to look out of the window. I turned my head and saw the most beautiful full arched rainbow that I had ever seen. I knew then that the angels had been helping to ensure a tranquil day to lay my mother to rest.

On the 23rd of November 2007 Dave was feeling very ill. He had a fever and felt both intensely hot and then freezing cold and was shivering. I phoned the emergency doctor and he said it sounded like a virus and just to give him plenty of fluids. I did as the doctor instructed but Dave still seemed very ill the following day so I phoned the emergency doctor again. I spoke to somebody different this time but I was given the same response although he told me to keep an eye on him because of his diabetes. By the 25th of November Dave seemed to be getting much worse and was looking desperately ill. His pillows and bedding were drenched with sweat and I could tell that something was seriously wrong with him. I called the emergency doctor once again at 11pm to receive the same advice again but by 1:00am I decided to take matters in to my own hands and called for an ambulance. After assessing Dave's condition the paramedics rushed him to the hospital and he was admitted in to intensive care. An abscess and ulcer on his foot had become infected and as a result he had developed septicaemia. This is a serious life threatening disease caused by bacteria getting in to the blood stream and poisoning it. The outlook for patients with septicaemia is dependent on the type of bacteria involved but the death rate for some of these is over 50% so we were all extremely worried. Dave's kidney's were failing and his blood pressure was dangerously low and he needed an operation on his foot. He was hooked up to a machine to monitor his vital organs and given antibiotics to treat the infection, fluids via an intravenous drip and given oxygen. One of the main problems with treating septicaemia is the doctors have to take blood cultures and find out which drugs or combination of drugs are effective in treating this particular form of blood poisoning. The whole process can take several days, meanwhile Dave was fighting for his life in intensive care. Eventually the correct combination of drugs was found for Dave and we just had to wait and see how his body reacted to it. When Dave regained consciousness after the operation he was in a state of total confusion and didn't recognise me or the rest of our family. It was very frightening not to mention heartbreaking to see someone you love seeming so lost and still in such a dangerously ill condition. The doctors told me that they were very concerned about how confused Dave had become and how long this confusion had lasted for, as many days had passed without improvement. As I sat in the waiting room I called upon Archangel Michael and I asked for strength and to be filled with a peaceful energy to help me cope with the situation.

I felt the energy surrounding me and filling me with peace, which despite everything happening around me was a wonderful feeling. I then called upon Archangel Raphael to send healing energy to Dave and asked for his confusion to leave him. The next morning when I went to visit Dave he had been taken out of intensive care and moved to a regular ward and was no longer in danger. He was no longer confused and I was able to speak with him properly for the first time since he became ill. One week later Dave had been discharged from hospital much to our family's great relief. I believe that if you ask and pray to God and the angels for help in situations like this, and if it is in the person's best interests, then your prayers will be answered.

Archangels have helped me a lot in my life. Their guidance support and love has helped me through many difficult times and made sure that I stay on the right path. If ever I have uncertainties in my life I will call upon the archangels for their advice. They are just waiting for you to ask them to help. They cannot do anything to help you unless you ask them first. Archangel is derived from Greek and literally translates as 'Chief Angel'. They represent the highest rank of angels and supervise angels and guardian angels. Each archangel has specialist skills and qualities so you can call on different archangels depending on your requirements. No wish is too small to call for help and an Archangel will never be too busy to answer you.

Archangel Michael is the angel to call upon when you need protection or have fears and his name means 'who is god like'. This is usually interpreted as a rhetorical question and represents humility before god, suggesting that no one is God like. I always ask Archangel Michael for protection for myself and my family every single morning. I visualise each person with a white light all around them, protecting them. I also put a protective light around the family car and ask that the car does not hit another car, object or person, and that no car, object or person will hit their car. I also ask archangel Michael to help guide people to and from their destination safely when they are travelling. You can also visualise a white light surrounding your house to protect your home, possessions and all that dwell in it. Personally I ask Archangel Michael to release any fears or negative energy from me, and ask for his strength, courage, peace and faith to flow through me. Archangel Michael can remove the negative energy from any space or situation both internal and in homes, or places of work. You can also imagine yourself covered by a purple cloak with the hood up for protection if you are scared or have fears. Purple and blue are the colours connected with Archangel Michael.

Archangel Raphael is the angel of healing and his name means 'God heals'. He helps people who are healers or committed to health care as well as those in need of healing. Archangel Raphael can also heal your mind from any negative beliefs that may trigger ill health. Archangel Raphael teaches us that we can heal ourselves through love and joy. If you are ill it stems from a lack of love in an aspect of your life, perhaps through anger, jealousy or another negative emotion. To heal yourself you must replace these negative emotions with love. Someone who is full of love will never get sick. I always call upon him before performing healing for someone. I ask for Archangel Raphael's green healing energy to flow through the person that I am healing and I ask for his guidance as I give the healing. If you or someone you know is having an operation then you can call upon Archangel Raphael to guide the surgeon's hand and that the treatment will be successful. You can also ask for Archangel Raphael's healing energy to flow through you if you are injured or ill so that you will heal more quickly. It is always important to thank the Archangel for the help that you are given. The colour connected with Archangel Raphael is emerald green.

Archangel Metatron is the patron of children and God's scribe, writing down all the things that happen in heaven. He is also often referred to as the angel of thought and is associated with the ability to manipulate time and space. Archangel Metatron is the mouth piece for God and provides a link between God and mankind. His name means 'he who walks with God' and has also been said to sit upon a throne next to God. You can ask archangel Metatron to help with looking after your children and to advise you the best action to take if your children are being very overly energetic or unruly. He is also a very good time keeper and if you are running late for an appointment you can ask him to help you meet all your train connections on time or that the traffic is not so busy so you will not arrive late. Archangel Metatron can also help you find balance in your life. Whether it is helping you to find an appropriate work/life balance, or telling you when you have done enough and need to stop. He can also tell you when you need to do more either for yourself or for others around you. It is believed that Archangel Metatron was once a human named Enoch who was a prophet. God took Enoch to heaven and turned him in to the Archangel Metatron. The colour connected to archangel Metatron is green with dark pink.

Archangel Chamuel is the angel of love and his name means 'he who sees God'. He is associated with love and peace and can help to expand your heart chakra to allow you to be more open to giving and receiving love and improve your loving relationships with others. You can also call upon archangel Chamuel to help you find lost objects or to discover your life's purpose. He can assist you in finding your soul mate, new friends or a new job if you ask him to. He can also provide you with peace of mind. Archangel Chamuel is connected to the colour pale green.

Archangel Gabriel is the messenger angel between God and humans and his name means 'God is my Strength'. Archangel Gabriel told Mary of the forthcoming arrival of Jesus and as a result is often referred to as the bearer of good news. He is seen by all religions as God's most powerful messenger delivering His word. Archangel Gabriel will help you with all forms of communication and helps journalists, writers and teachers. I myself, have asked Archangel Gabriel for his help in writing this book. If you are about to give a speech or attend a meeting ask archangel Gabriel for help in finding the right words to say. Archangel Gabriel embraces our individuality and guides us to the right path to help us to find our own personal truths and encourages us to nurture our God-given talents and express ourselves fully. Archangel Gabriel also helps couples trying to conceive or to adopt a child, and helps mother's through pregnancy and guides children through the early years of their life. You can also call upon Archangel Gabriel to assist you in any kind of new ventures such as moving home or starting a new job or business. The colour connected to archangel Gabriel is dark yellow.

Like Archangel Metatron, Archangel Sandalphon is believed to have human origins as the prophet Elijah and they are often described at twin brothers, his name actually means 'brother'. Archangel Sandalphon guides people in prayer and creativity particularly in terms of music and focuses on helping people develop personal growth, including helping teachers to guide their students creatively. Archangel Sandalphon helps people to use their thoughts, emotions and prayers in their creative projects and acts as a muse to creative people. Musicians, singers and people working within music therapy can call upon Archangel Sandalphon for guidance in expressing themselves creatively. The colour connected to Archangel Sandalphon is turquoise.

Archangel Uriel is the angel of peace and his name means 'God is my light'. It was archangel Uriel who was sent to earth to warn Noah of the forthcoming floods. He helps you to focus your mind and provides inspiration to help you solve problems and improve your memory. Archangel Uriel also helps to heal troubled relationships and resolve conflicts peacefully. He provides you with a strong foundation of love to enable you to come to terms with negative moments from your past and find forgiveness for yourself and others. He helps us understand karmic laws and that sometimes bad things happen in our lives in order to bring a greater joy at a later point. Whenever you feel as if you have lost your way Archangel Uriel can help to provide the knowledge you need to find the right path. The colour associated with Archangel Uriel is pale yellow.

Archangel Jophiel is the angel of enlightenment and his name means 'beauty of God', he teaches us about the importance of beauty within, as well as physical beauty. Archangel Jophiel understands that not everyone is happy with their appearance or our clothes and that this can prevent us from feeling confident about ourselves. In order to give out love we also need to be able to love ourselves within and he can help us with this if we ask him. Archangel Jophiel encourages us to think beautiful thoughts and focus on the light within ourselves and as a result attract more beauty in to our lives. Archangel Jophiel helps us with retaining information and is the angel to call upon if you are studying for an exam, or need to concentrate on something. He also helps us to develop our intuition, awareness and freedom of thought, providing us with flashes of inspiration. It is said that Archangel Jophiel was the angel who cast Adam and Eve from the garden of Eden. The colour associated with Archangel Jophiel is fuchsia.

Archangel Azrael is the angel of death and his name means 'who God helps'. Archangel Azrael helps people to accept death and to let go of this world and not to anchor themselves to earth after their death. He safely guides their souls in the journey from earth to heaven and ensures that this transition is peaceful and that people adjust to their new life in heaven. Archangel Azrael also offers comfort and help to people to heal from grief after losing a loved one. You can call upon Archangel Azrael if you have recently lost someone or need help coming to terms with losing someone. He offers guidance to grief counsellors and those who offer spiritual guidance to others. Archangel Azrael is associated with the colour beige.

Archangel Ariel is the angel of nature and is strongly linked with the natural elements Earth, Air, Water and Fire. Archangel Ariel can appear in either male or female form and whose name means 'lion of God'. Archangel Ariel helps people who are interested in nature, animals and the environment. You can ask for help with taking care of the environment, conservation projects or for healing animals, both wild and domesticated. Archangel Ariel aims to help rid us of fearful thoughts and beliefs and to understand that our limitations are merely illusions and that our future accomplishments can be truly without limits if we believe it to be so. We can only achieve miracles if we believe that it is possible. Archangel Ariel can also help people with expenses related to their life purpose. One day when I was very short of money I asked for a small amount of money to help meet my needs. Shortly afterwards I walked out of my front door and a ten pound note blew across the ground in front of my feet. There wasn't a sole in sight and I think it was meant for me so I thanked Archangel Ariel for this gift. The colour associated with Archangel Ariel is pale pink.

Archangel Haniel is the angel of joy and grace and his name means 'grace of God'. He appears in female form more often than male, usually appearing as a beautiful woman. Archangel Haniel offers guidance to people who want to develop their spiritual growth, intuition and psychic abilities. He may guide you to certain books, classes or teachers in order for you to develop your skills. Archangel Haniel believes that we are all inherently psychic and can help to push our psychic abilities to our conscious mind. He will also help you if you wish to use crystals to improve health or healing. Archangel Haniel symbolises love, peace, beauty and friendship and if you feel that your life is incomplete in any way or that you are going through a period of sadness then you can call upon Archangel Haniel to assist you and help you find happiness. Archangel Haniel can also help you to be graceful on any occasion where you may need to be, for example while being interviewed for a job, in a meeting, giving a performance or presentation, or when trying to make a good impression with someone. The colour connected to Archangel Haniel is light blue.

Archangel Zadkiel is the angel of forgiveness and mercy and is also associated with freedom and benevolence. His name means 'the righteousness of God'. Archangel Zadkiel heals painful memories and enables you to forgive others. In turn this releases you from the burden of anger and bitterness of the negative events of your past, by directing your thoughts to beautiful memories and positive thoughts. He enables you to look upon others and their actions with compassion and without judgement. You can also call upon Archangel Zadkiel if you have done something wrong and you wish to be forgiven, or in times of spiritual doubt. Archangel Zadkiel also helps to improve our memories and is of great benefit to students. The colour associated with Archangel Zadkiel is dark blue.

Guided by Angels

Archangel Raphael
A story to tell,

Of an emerald green healing light
Flashing sparks, a divine sight
Guides and protectors watching everyone
Healing the earth, under the sun

Still the mind and you will find
An inner peace, so soft, so kind
A healing energy, to calm your fears
A divine light, throughout the years
Guiding you along your chosen path
Bringing joy, a smile, a laugh

A warm glow, a comforting feeling
A reviving energy of emotional healing
Pulsating colours from a far
Shining down as a bright star

A kaleidoscope of colours
Of angels and their brothers
Clarifying your faith, hopes and dreams
With visions and insights, thoughts and themes
A vibrating energy when they appear
A sweet music for all to hear
Releasing toxins and negativity
Leaving a feeling of serenity

Feeling whole, being at one
Like golden rays beneath the sun
Sparkling with a vivacity

Filled with a new vitality

Emerald green healing light
Flashing sparks, a divine sight
Guides and protectors watching everyone
Healing the earth, under the sun

Angel Lights

Archangel Michael shimmering through
A golden glow
Like diamonds in the snow
A vision of sparkling angel lights
An aura of orbs, a soulful sight
A cloak of blue and purple light
Guarding you through silent nights

An energy of love and peace
A sign of joy and release
A presence to behold
Miracles to be told

Of courage and protection
Of love and reflection
Intervening to make you safe
A guardian angel full of faith

A sword held high
Towards the sky
A powerful energy, a protective love
A vision of healing, from above

I believe that there are many different ways that we can receive messages from the angels and one of the other techniques that I use is to look in to my crystal ball. Many times when I have looked in to my crystal ball I do not see anything at all. I do not think it is realistic to see something every time that I look at it. Sometimes the things that you see cannot be taken too literally as images of things to come, and should instead be viewed as a message that may not make immediate sense to you. One morning when looking in my crystal ball I saw my golden retriever 'Merlin' and next to him was a mound of earth with a cross on it that looked like a small grave. I became very worried by what I had seen. I told several people about it and they said that Merlin was perfectly healthy so there was no need to worry. A week later our old next door neighbour came to visit my mother-in-law completely out of the blue. She was now living in a rented flat and needed someone to look after her dog because she wasn't allowed to keep him there. My mother-in-law had always loved dogs and had many as pets over the years, so she was happy to look after him. The dog was very old and sadly after a happy week of looking after him he passed away. It was very upsetting for my mother-in-law, as she had only just begun looking after the dog and bonding with him. Sometimes when we see things in a crystal ball we are presented with familiar images to explain what is going to happen, rather than the literal meaning. Merlin was just a familiar image to me to represent a dog and the mound of earth with a cross represented the dog that died. The surprising thing was that at the time of me looking in to the crystal ball and receiving the message we had no idea that my mother-in-law would be looking after someone's dog.

If you have a crystal ball and would like to know how to use it, you should start by holding it in your hands and looking deep in to the ball noticing the multitude of colours refracted as light hits the occlusions. Focus on particular point that looks like a gap or opening in the occlusions that you can look through. Don't stare too intensely at the crystal ball, you need to be in a completely tranquil state of mind as if daydreaming or just staring in to space. A good time to try this is after meditating when you are feeling peaceful and relaxed. Spend no longer than ten minutes at a time and restrict yourself to looking in to the crystal ball just once a day when you are starting out as a beginner. When symbols or images come to you it is up to you to interpret the meaning as it will not necessarily be a straight-forward vision of the future. It is always important to take good care of your crystal ball. If you wish to re-energise the crystal ball place it in the sunlight and if you want to clean it place it in the moonlight. It does not actually have to be outside, placing it on a windowsill is perfectly fine. It is important that nobody touches your crystal ball apart from you otherwise that person's energy will be transferred on to it and it should only be connected to your energy in order for you to be able to use it. If someone does touch your crystal ball you should clean it first and then re-energise it.

On the 26th of November 2009 Dave decided to write out all of the Christmas cards to send out to our family and friends. He had recently learned how to use the internet and send emails and he very much enjoyed being able to do this. Dave did all the Christmas shopping for presents online for our boys, our daughter-in-law Teenie and our grandson Joshua. He wanted everything to be perfect for Christmas time. We were especially excited this year as Taro and Teenie were expecting another baby and we couldn't wait to see our second grandson. The baby was not due until April but it was impossible not to get excited about the new arrival. Joshua had brought so much love in to our family's life and we were looking forward to experiencing that joy all over again. It had been a busy day as we had also walked around town picking up items for Christmas. Dave was in a really happy mood and he seemed healthier than he had been for some time. Every evening Dave would use an exercise bike as he was very dedicated to losing some weight and improving his health. Dave went upstairs to exercise and I watched TV with Barry in the front room. About thirty minutes later we heard a loud bang. We both rushed upstairs to see what had happened. I feared that Dave may have slipped in the bathroom because of the difficulties he had with his balance. We arrived to find Dave lying unconscious on the bedroom floor. We tried calling out to him but it made no difference. We phoned for an ambulance and I performed CPR but we could not revive him. The paramedics arrived and worked on Dave for over an hour and all Barry and I could do was watch and pray. They continued to perform CPR and use a defibrillator in the ambulance on the way to the hospital. As we arrived Barry and I were taken to a small waiting room while the paramedics rushed Dave inside to receive further treatment. About ten minutes later a doctor came to tell us that they had done all they could. Dave had been pronounced dead. The shock was unbearable. I needed to see Dave to say one last goodbye while Barry phoned Taro to tell him what had happened. It is amazing how your life can just spin out of control in a matter of moments. Just hours before we had been so happy together. You can never take life for granted because you really have no idea what is waiting for you around the corner. We arrived home feeling empty and broken. Barry broke the news to my mother-in-law. Tragically she had now outlived both of her sons. The three of us sat on the sofa together, held each other and cried. There was really nothing left to say. The following morning Taro, Teenie and Joshua travelled up from London and it was a great comfort to me in the most difficult time of my life. Although I prayed for Dave to survive I understand that this must just have been his time. I believe that before we are born we make an agreement on the life we have, the lessons that we need to learn and the time that we will die. I believe that it is so much harder for the people left behind because when you die, your spirit lives on and it is like you are returning home. I know I will see Dave again when the time is right for me to join him.

Sacred White Lion

An African lion so pure, so white
An aura glowing bright and light
Love radiating from his soul at night
Spreading peace a powerful sight
A star of Orion
A sacred white lion
The law of the jungle, a King
People chant and sing

A ghostly glow in the distance
Roaming free with no resistance
Each paw slowly advancing
As if he was prancing and dancing
A slow and even pace
Each step calmly in place

Born to be free
A spirit of energy, for all to see
A wisdom for all to connect
A higher consciousness to protect
Radiating a healing energy, an ecstasy
Glowing white rays like a fantasy

As white as the snow
Watching regally as he grows
An African white lion, so pure, so white
As he gazes out, across the night
A star of Orion
A sacred white lion
Jutting out his jaw
With an explosive roar
Echoing through the trembling ground

A peaceful energy a courageous sound
Head held high, looking proud
A mystical figure, through a cloud
A mystery for all to see
A sacred white lion beneath a tree

A presence full of wisdom
As he watches over his Kingdom
A miracle of the wild
A flowing energy that's mild
A breath escapes like a sigh
As crystals flow from the sky
Sparks falling from his tail
As he swishes it like a sail

About five months after Dave had passed away my second grandson was born, Lucas David Russell. I was very touched that Taro and Teenie had decided to use Dave's name as Lucas' middle name. He was so looking forward to seeing Lucas. Thankfully the birth was much easier on Teenie this time around. I asked the angels to be with her and to ease her pain and for the baby to be born healthy. Teenie gave birth in a birthing pool, listening to a CD made up of all her favourite songs. Out of all the songs that were on the CD it was the song that she and Taro danced to on their wedding that was being played as Lucas entered the world. I believe that this was a sign that the angels were watching over her. When Lucas was born everybody said how much he looked like Dave, which pleased me as Dave did not live to see him. Lucas does not look like Joshua at all as he has a much paler complexion, with very blonde hair and beautiful blue eyes just like his dad.

It was about a year after Dave died that his mother Marjorie started displaying strange behaviour. She would often get her words muddled up when she spoke, so I took her to see the doctor. After a few trips to the hospital and several scans it was revealed that she had a large brain tumour that was inoperable. Her speech had become much more confused but the doctor prescribed some medicine that reduced the swelling on her brain and improved her speech greatly, although only temporarily. The doctor explained to me that she was terminally ill and she may have only weeks or months left to live. My mother-in-law has always been extremely strong willed and independent but as her condition worsened I took care of her more and more. Eventually her condition became so bad that she could no longer get up from a sitting position on her own anymore and I couldn't lift her to help her. She had carers that would come to see her every day and help out but she would often refuse their help as she has always done everything for herself in the past. Unfortunately this made things very hard for me and it was becoming increasingly apparent that she needed someone who could care for her twenty four hours a day. She had many falls and as a result needed to go in to hospital. It was at this time that I realised that I could no longer look after her any more. After discussing the matter with Marjorie and her other daughter-in-law Heather, we agreed that the only option was to find a nursing home who could give her the care that she needed. Sadly a week after moving in to her new home she passed away. During the months that she was ill she didn't want me to give her any healing, as I think she had accepted what was happening to her and didn't want the process to be drawn out. So instead I asked the angels that if it was her time, then to please not let her linger and suffer and thankfully she did not.

Every morning I close my eyes and ask archangel Michael for protection for myself and for all of my family, and take some time to meditate. After Dave had passed away I had put my house up for sale as it was too big for me and it now held very sad memories of losing him. Tragically within a three year period I had to cope with the illness and passing of my husband, my mother, and my mother-in-law. The house had been up for sale for over a year and I was doubting that it would ever sell, so I asked archangel Michael for his help to get our house sold so I could move on to some where new. Archangel Michael replied to me that I would be moving soon but I needed to think more positively about the move and believe that it was actually happening. He told me that negative thoughts only cause delays in getting want you really want. He also told me that there is no such thing as coincidence, that everything happens for a reason and what is meant to happen will happen. I said to archangel Michael how can I be sure that this is your voice that I am hearing and not just my own inner voice or thoughts. He replied by telling me to pick up my deck of Unicorn cards and split the pack without shuffling them. After I had finished meditating I picked up my unicorn cards and split the pack as I had been told, which revealed to me the archangel Michael card. After this I truly believed that I was talking directly to archangel Michael. It can be so easy to dismiss what you hear from the angels as your own thoughts. When meditating you may find it useful to focus on listening to what may seem like your thoughts, then after-wards make notes and read them back to yourself later.

There are other types of angels that you can communicate

with in addition to the archangels. Every person has their own guardian angels, assigned by God, to guide them through life offering protection and advice. If you have ever had a gut feeling about something that is usually your guardian angel offering you advice on which path to take. The notion of guardian angels is a common one throughout religious beliefs and ancient Greek philosophy, and has been included in works from Pseudo-Dionysius the Areopagite's work on celestial hierarchy to Plato's Phaedo. Potentially your guardian angel can be someone from almost any background, which may be entirely dissimilar to your own. The crucial factor is in matching how spiritual a person is with a guardian angel of equal spirituality. I didn't intentionally set out to make contact with my guardian angel, it felt more like something that happened to me rather than something I sought out. I was lying in bed meditating with my eyes closed when I saw a moving picture of a Buddhist monk sitting on a large boulder. He had a very kind looking face and as he turned to face me he gave me a beautiful smile. I asked him what his name was and in my mind I received the answer 'Tao-Chi Ling'. I was very pleased to have met him. Then this image cleared and I saw a Native Indian in full headdress. He told me that his name was Chief Sharana and the name Gerimeo also came to me, although I do not know the significance of this. Now I feel like my guardian angels are friends that I can ask for help when I am healing someone and I feel very lucky to have them in my life. It is not uncommon for people with strong spirituality to have guardian angels such as Native Americans or Monks because these groups of people led very spiritual lives and therefore are a perfect match. It is not the background that is significant in determining who your guardian angel will be but their level of spirituality and their bond to you.

Although I was fortunate enough to have my guardian angels approach me this is not how it usually works for most people. One way to encourage conversation with your guardian angel is to focus on the seven levels that make up the aura body. The first aura level is the Etheric level which is half an inch to two inches away from the body. It has a silver/hazy white colour and is related to the root chakra and as a result can be seen as the colour red when it is clear. The second aura level is the emotional level which is one to three inches away from the body and is more fluid than the Etheric level. This level is associated with feelings and is linked to the astral layer. This level relates to the sacral chakra and resonates orange when it is clear. The third aura level is the mental level which is three to eight inches from the body. This level is associated with thoughts and mental processes. This is the level that you can connect with deceased loved ones through your thoughts and dreams and ask for reassurance, as when I saw my father after he had died, just for a few seconds to let me know that he was alright. As you develop further awareness with this level the more you will be able to connect with more deceased loved ones and past lives. This level is connected to the solar-plexus chakra and resonates as a golden yellow colour around the head and shoulders when it is clear. The fourth aura level is the astral level and is six inches to a foot from the body. This is where you channel healing energies from higher planes. It is through this level that with meditation you can meet your spirit guides. This level is connected to the heart chakra and resonates to the colour green. The fifth aura level is the Etheric template body and on this level there is a copy of your physical body which is eighteen inches to two feet from your actual body. Energy on this level operates on a higher spiritual vibration than the previous levels and it is the first of the higher aura levels. It is on this level, during higher meditation techniques, that archangels and masters can be found and communicated with. This level is linked to the throat chakra and resonates to the colour sky blue. When your chakras are completely balanced it is through this level that you may feel a sense of oneness and contentment with the world. The sixth aura level, and the second of the higher levels, is the celestial body, which is two feet to two feet nine inches from the body. This level is where you can see spirit guides and angels more clearly and when you can connect to these cosmic energies and the higher angels you will receive wisdom from a higher source. The celestial plane is connected to the third eye chakra and resonates to the colour indigo. The seventh level, and the final of the three higher levels, is the causal body, which is two and a half feet to three and a half feet from the body. This is the spiritual layer that is at the highest level and by raising our awareness on this level we can become at one with God. This level is connected to the crown chakra and resonates to the colours violet, white and gold. If you focus on these seven layers of aura colours when meditating you can clear both your aura and your energy centre and also stimulate a connection with your guardian angels. Visualise the red aura surrounding you, and then imagine the orange aura layered over this and then in turn the yellow aura layered over the top of that, until you are visualising the seven layers of colour surrounding your body. Once each of these aura levels are cleared and vibrating at a higher frequency this will increase your ability to make contact with your guardian angel and your capability of hearing them when they have a message for you. It is believed that the higher aura levels form the soul and it is through these that we can communicate with beings of a higher spiritual order. After this try to speak to your guardian angel as you would speak to one of your friends. You can ask their name and details about them and the responses will come to you in the form of your thoughts or dreams. There is no certain way of knowing how long it may take before you can commune with your guardian angels. It can happen very quickly for some people where as it can take years of practice for others. It is not something that you can force, it all depends on whether you are spiritually and emotionally ready to take the next step or when you are at a time in your life to be able to commit the time required for this.

After a long time waiting, my house in Weston-Super-Mare was finally sold to a nice couple with three children. All the time leading up to this I was viewing other houses but none of them that I had seen felt right. So I asked the angels to guide me to the right property. I explained that I was looking for a home with lots of trees near it and that I would love to be able to hear the birds singing. I also asked the angels to help me find a house that had a conservatory so that I could set up a healing practice. Barry had been making all the arrangements of selling our house and trying to find houses in a new area for me to view. I wanted to live nearer to Taro, Teenie and my grandchildren so Barry found five houses for me to view in Bracknell, Berkshire, which was only a thirty minute drive away from them. The very first house that we saw excited me because it met all of our requirements and had a good 'feeling' about it. I also loved the second house we saw which had a slightly more modern look about it. I made an offer for the second house, even though it was more money than I could really afford, but it was turned down anyway as the property owner had just raised the price from what she was originally prepared to accept. Straight after hearing the news Barry then searched the internet and found that the first house we had looked at had just been reduced in price by five thousand pounds that morning. This put the house in to a more realistic price bracket for me. So I made an offer on the house which was accepted just a few minutes later. After so long trying to find the right home the deal went through in such a short space of time. In hindsight I felt very lucky that my initial offer was rejected. I believe that the angels were helping me as the same morning that I was turned down from one property, the other house was reduced in price. Whenever I used to give healing to Dave he would always say that he visualised looking up in to very tall trees, which was strange as we didn't really know anywhere like that. Since moving in to my home these words came in to my mind as my house is right next to a small forest and is surrounded by tall trees. People might dismiss it as coincidence, but I have never been one to believe in coincidence. I believe that Dave was seeing the tall trees that surround my house and that I was guided to this home by angels.

Eclipse of the Moon

An eclipse of the moon
From morning to noon
In shades of blackness
A sky that's sunless
As silent trees sway
And shadows slip away
The moon orbits the earth
As the sun rises to give birth

As the moon's surface disappears
Through clouds of mystery reappears
Falling into an inky space
Escaping across the human race
Revealing a shifting in time
Silently looking up in mime
A woven grid of energy lines
Guiding you with secret signs

When an angel appears
The ebony sky clears
Each turn creating another direction
Helping you make the right connection
A path to follow, showing you the way
Shadows of dark kept at bay
Smiling through the storm
A new light is born

A muted voice
That needs a choice
Swallowing all thought of wrong
As the light makes you strong
Breaking through a dim lit day

To a light reflecting in a special way

Seeing through a mist
Eyes focussed, can't resist
Drifting like sand
Shielded by a sweeping hand
Peeping into rays of colour
Trying gently not to smother
From rays of light, your eyes to cover

Watching over a flying swallow
Guiding you into another tomorrow
As the birds believe that day is night
They seem to give up without a fight
Silently falling into a sleep
Bumping about into a heap
As the birds waken into a new song
Rejoicing sounds as you walk along

Stretching across a forbidden Kingdom
Channelling into a hidden wisdom
Across the moon's face
Looking smooth, without a trace
Are valleys and mountains
Reflections of sunshine like fountains
Looking into the reason of time
A moon in all its prime
A new future wins
As a new day begins

An eclipse of the moon.

When an angel comes in to your life you feel peace and tranquility. You feel a sense of awareness that your life has a strong meaning. Your life is a journey from the first day to the last and it is up to you to decide which path you will take. There are many hurdles that you will have to face on this journey, but each obstacle you overcome brings you a step closer to your soul's purpose. It is important to follow your own path and face life's challenges head on and not run away from them. It is by conquering our fears and the difficulties that we face in life that will eventually lead to enlightenment, which is a feeling of being at one with yourself, feeling balanced and whole. Every step we take towards attaining our goals brings us closer to fulfillment. We spend our entire life learning lessons and for some it can take many lifetimes before you have learned all that you need to before you can move on from this world. This is why some people experience déjà vu when meeting new people or visiting certain places, they have actually had these experiences before, but in a different life. As we travel through life meeting new people and making new friends, we are actually reacquainting ourselves with old friends from previous lives. The ties between us are never really broken. How many times have you heard someone say "have we met before? You look so familiar". People also talk about how coincidences occur all the time, but life is not full of coincidences or chance occurrences, only things that are meant to happen to us on our journey. All of our previous lives are linked together so that we do not have to re-learn lessons or make the same mistakes again. Every single particle of the world, invisible to the naked eye, forms part of our past, present and future. Each person's story is linked together and our life has a ripple affect that impacts on people all over the world. This is true of both positive and negative energy, if we give out positive energy then we can change the atmosphere around us and the people who we come in to contact with. Our thought patterns impact on all of those around us and we can feel the positive or negative energy in a situation without a word being spoken. Our thought patterns are a form of intuition and it is this gut instinct that tells us how to deal with a problem or difficult situation, by listening to your innermost thoughts the answers will come to you. It is in these moments of instinct that our guardian angels are trying to help us to make the right decisions. Everyone has a guardian angel and they want to help us but cannot have a direct impact on our life unless they are invited to do so. They are waiting to help us but first we have to ask them for help and then tune in to them and listen to their advice. We all have dreams and these dreams often have a basis in reality, such as overcoming a fear or achieving a goal that seems just out of reach. It is important to try and fulfill these ambitions as doing so makes your soul rejoice and this is how we can achieve long term happiness and joy. Heaven is much like being on earth except that you no longer have a solid body, but are instead made up of energy. You can do all the same things that you could do on earth and you are still learning, however you are much wiser at this point and have grown spiritually. You no longer face the same problems as you did on earth because you realise that they are not that important anymore and everything becomes clearer to you now. There are still good and bad souls just like on earth, but the bad souls are just lost and they will eventually find their way.

Why, when there is so much help available to us from the angels, do we not all grasp the opportunity with both hands? All you have to do is ask for their assistance. As stated earlier on, by getting to know the angels we can learn who to contact depending on our requirements. Taking in to account all of these factors it is strange that we can be too afraid to take chances in life, considering the amount of help that is available to us. The reason that this occurs is that we doubt ourselves and our abilities. When the first people were on earth, before any common language was invented, they trusted each other because they had to. It was essential in terms of gathering food and surviving. Throughout the years as mankind has developed we have become more independent, making our own decisions and not relying on each other, which has put a distance between us all. It is only in times of crisis when people are brought together that these bonds are reunited. As someone approaches the end of their time on earth their life still has meaning. All the trials of life only serve to make us stronger and are part of the learning process, no matter how big or small the meanings are to you. Each change throughout our lives, whether good or bad, is a step forwards. When was the last time that you sat down and thought about what you have achieved with your life. It does not matter how small the good deeds you do are, for example helping someone with their shopping or putting a smile on someone's face, as they will send ripples out across the ocean of life. In order to send love out in to the world it is first important to love yourself, if you don't how can you expect anybody else to.

I would like to end this book with a message that came to me from one of my spirit guides: Tao-Chi Ling. 'My life as a Buddhist monk was hard at the beginning. The ability to meditate and feel the energy all around you and flowing through you, and contemplating on the world, did not come to me in a few minutes. It took a great deal of practice, just like all things you wish to achieve in life, you have to work hard at it. In time, everything comes naturally to you, with each breath that you take your energy flows with it and every step you take becomes calm. Eventually your whole body is meditating not just your mind, as the energy also flows through your body and spirit, like a pebble thrown in to a pond, each ripple connecting us, as we connect to each other. When walking through a wood take time to look at the leaves on the trees, breathe in the fresh smell of the grass, see the birds that follow along your path. All aspects of nature and animals are trying to show you signs that you do not take any notice of as you are too caught up in the events of your day. Too busy to look up and see how wonderful and beautiful nature really is. All of this is around you all of the time and is free. Why not take one day at a time as if each day is new. Still dream your dreams and turn them in to reality by imagining every detail and seeing yourself reaching your goals. By visualising these dreams becoming real in your mind they will become real in your life. Fear is not fear itself but the negative thoughts that you apply to a situation, which always makes the situation seem much worse than it really is. So instead of worrying about something think about yourself in a positive way. For example when going to the dentist, the fear is far worse than the treatment itself. It's very easy for someone to tell you not to worry but it is something that you can train yourself to do. Imagine what your life would be like if you accepted a situation for what it is and did not have the build-up of fear to overcome. In order to do this you have to focus on living in the now and stop your mind from racing forwards, just take each moment as it comes and don't worry about what will happen. If you smile at life, life will smile back at you.'

'Have you ever felt that you are trapped, as if a fence were surrounding you and there is no escape. All you have to do is open the gate and set yourself free. Nobody is doing this to you, it is just your own thoughts. Just believe that you are in charge of your own mind and if you don't want to think negative thoughts then don't. You are in charge of your own thoughts, not the other way around. You must keep telling yourself not to think negative thoughts and instead replace them with positive thoughts. If you feel that life is passing you by then it is up to you not to let it, this is a very special life that you have. Focus on living in the moment and only planning one day at a time. Set yourself a goal for each day no matter how small it is. Even just writing down a thought for the day that was special to you. It can be as small as going for a walk, seeing a robin, or a special flower or the way that the clouds are formed across the sky. It doesn't have to be big life changing moments that you write about, just small things that you see but do not normally take notice of.'

AYNI
BOOKS

"Ayni" is a Quechua word meaning "reciprocity" – sharing, giving and receiving – whatever you give out comes back to you. To be in Ayni is to be in balance, harmony and right relationship with oneself and nature, of which we are all an intrinsic part. Complementary and Alternative approaches to health and well-being essentially follow a holistic model, within which one is given support and encouragement to move towards a state of balance, true health and wholeness, ultimately leading to the awareness of one's unique place in the Universal jigsaw of life – Ayni, in fact.